POWERLIFT

**BILL
ASHPAUGH**
with
Holly Miller

**impact
books**

A division of The Benson Company, Inc.
Nashville, Tennessee

Catalog Number: 14013p

Ashpaugh, Bill.
    Powerlift.

        1. Ashpaugh, Bill.   2. Weight lifters—United States—
Biography. I. Miller, Holly. II. Title.
GV545.52.A8A36   796.4'1 [B]   80-81758
ISBN 0-914850-67-9   AACR2

Dedicated to

God

Mom and Dad

Brothers and Sisters

Wife, Nancy

and

to all the people who helped make this book possible

CONTENTS

INTRODUCTION:
HIS TOWN

Ask any resident of Noblesville, Indiana, to tell his favorite Bill Ashpaugh story and first you'll get a grin and then you'll get a memory. Not that Bill is someone from the past . . . far from it. But he *is* something of a legend in this sprawling Hoosier town where hulking Victorian homes drip gingerbread over narrow, shady sidewalks, and the local hamburger palace exchanges neon winks with the "veddy" expensive British steak house across the highway.

To know Noblesville is to understand Bill. Although he isn't a native—he came here by way of Westfield, by way of Zionsville—he and his adopted hometown have much in common. They both have the knack of blending the old-fashioned and the new-fangled, somehow managing to extract the best of each world and discard the rest. They can latch onto trends without forgetting their roots. They have the kind of charisma that draws young and old, rural and citified, blue-collar and professional, into their fold. Both Bill and his hometown share values that are throwbacks to another time—solid and unbudgeable—all wrapped up in a handsome, up-to-date package.

The city of Noblesville—population 11,634 and growing—has been on the map since 1851. Only recently has it been discovered by members of the Indianapolis work force looking for a quiet place to sleep, raise families, and enjoy weekend *R* and *R* after forty hours on the job in the state's capital. About five years ago, word got around that anyone willing to spend half an hour on the interstate would be amply rewarded with rolling green hills, good schools, great neighbors, and, yes, real trees. Noblesville? To weary city-dwellers, it seemed an oasis in a parched stretch of sand—a chunk of Kentucky that blew North and settled in the middle of the Indiana pavement.

Bill's been here much longer than the commuters, and he's watched his town blossom. With the influx of new citizens came change: Old store fronts were given facelifts, and when ladders and scaffolding were peeled away like bandages after surgery, the shops emerged as "shoppes" (*ye olde* variety) done up in brick, barnsiding, earth tones, and wrought iron. Assisting the metamorphosis was Bill himself, proprietor of Ashpaugh Construction Company. The company's office is at the center of town, located over the corner drugstore, looking down on all the activity.

From Bill's vantage point, Noblesville today reminds one of a stone tossed in a pool of water, sending out rings across a quiet surface. At the center is the huge courthouse, circa 1878, a looming brick and concrete box with twenty-foot ceilings and varnished oak woodwork. The inner ring is made up of the rambling old houses with wavy glass windowpanes, turrets, and shutters that really shut. The middle ring is new suburbia with split-level homes, two-car garages, total electric kitchens and let's-be-neighborly-but-not-too-neighborly chain link fences. The outer ring, stretching toward the cloverleaves and inner loop of Indianapolis, consists of condominiums and apartment complexes with their gas logs, circular floor plans and wall-to-wall Naughahyde game rooms.

Bill prefers the center, the hub of Noblesville, where the natives sit on park benches reading the *Evening Ledger* and complaining about the newcomers, while merchants drink coffee at the local lunch counter and give thanks for the boom in business. He's welcome in both places—on the bench and at the counter. Like a chameleon, he blends into his surroundings, always responding appropriately to the problem at hand. He's an optimist who comes on strong, but not too strong, and he never gives up. He's a fighter who once fought a big battle and won. All of Noblesville knows it and respects him for it.

When he's not in his second-floor office or visiting one of his construction sites around Hamilton County, Bill usually can be found at "his table" in the corner drugstore, greeting everyone by name and acting as listening post for the downtown regulars. Denny Hadley, owner and pharmacist, considers Bill one of the assets included in the property he purchased six years ago. He laughs as he recounts *his* favorite Bill Ashpaugh story, the one that involves the sale of a hundred or so hot-water bottles a year.

Shortly after Denny bought the pharmacy back in 1973, he noticed Bill was stopping in the store two or three times a week to buy rubber hot-water bottles. *Something is wrong,* decided Denny. Either the bottles he stocked were of poor quality or this massive bundle of human muscle had a mysterious medical problem that required constant application of heat. But even the most dedicated user of a hot-water bottle rarely needed a replacement more often than once a year. Finally, curiosity getting the best of him, Denny set aside his professional manner for a moment, and asked Bill point-blank what he was doing with two water bottles a week. Bill offered to *show* him instead.

In addition to being a homebuilder, he explained,

stretching a bottle first one way and then the other, he was a bodybuilder who presented programs on physical fitness and Christian witness around the country. Sometimes his audience was a Rotary Club or a Women's Aglow fellowship—attentive groups that were also gracious and appreciative. But more often he spoke to gatherings of teen-agers or even a "captive" audience of prison inmates who could be unruly and usually subscribed to a "show-me" philosophy. One of the best ways to show 'em was to gain their attention with an exhibition of strength, and follow through with a testimony about his spiritual convictions. A sure crowd-pleaser, guaranteed to win the respect of even the most unfriendly audience, was his feat of blowing air from his lungs into a hot-water bottle until it burst.

Enough said. Denny began doubling his order with the hot-water bottle supplier and he and Bill have been pals ever since.

Just down the street from the drugstore is the health spa owned and operated by Jeff Boze, himself a bodybuilder with a string of impressive titles to his credit. When Jeff came to Noblesville last year, one of his top priorities was to give Bill an open invitation to use his facility anytime, day or night. This gesture was extended partly out of friendship but primarily because he thinks Bill is a good influence in the gym. One of *his* favorite Ashpaugh memories dates back to February 1980, when an Indianapolis television crew came to the spa to film Bill pumping iron. Rather than using the TV exposure as an opportunity to promote himself, Bill saw it as a chance to boost his friends in the gym. During his workout he asked a young bodybuilder, new to the sport, to "spot" him while he bench pressed for the camera. No, Bill didn't really need a spotter to stand by in case he had trouble lowering the bar over his chest (it only weighed 130 pounds and he can lift 420) but he knew the excitement the youth would feel at seeing himself on national television. And that was important. Later, when he ducked into the dressing room to put on his sweatsuit for the interview portion of the show, he made sure his warmup jacket didn't hide the T-shirt he wore—the one that promoted Jeff's new gym.

Even at the height of his competitive sports career, Bill has always made time for beginners, the little guys who looked up to him as an example. Danny Godby first met Bill several years ago at a Noblesville service station where Bill and a mechanic were huddled under the hood of a truck trying to fix the engine. When a faulty steel rod was identified as the source of the problem, Bill reached in with one hand, broke it in half, and pulled it out. Simple? Not to Danny, an eighth-grader at the time, who decided on the spot that he wanted to grow up to be just like Bill. In many ways he has succeeded. He credits Bill with teaching him the sport of bodybuilding. Danny's mother goes further and claims Bill has served as a tremendous moral and spiritual influence on her son.

Danny's favorite Ashpaugh story took place in the snowy winter of '78, when Bill invited him to ride along to Toledo, Ohio, where he was scheduled to give a fitness-witness program to a group of young students. Danny was elated. The two had become close friends, had worked out together in the gym and had established a kind of mutual admiration society. Danny was proud of Bill's bodybuilding honors, and Bill boasted about Dan's many high school football accolades. The weather was so severe that night that they almost missed the program. A blizzard met them somewhere on the outskirts of Toledo and caused them to lose their bearings and slide off the road. They arrived at the auditorium late, but so did the audience. Because of the delay, Bill decided to give an abbreviated version of his

show. Still, some things can't be omitted. He took time
to introduce his friend Danny and to give a glowing
summary of the youth's All-State football career. At the
conclusion of the program, the audience clustered
around Bill *and* Dan for autographs. Bill had convinced
them they had two, not one, accomplished athletes in
their midst that night.

Such Ashpaugh stories aren't reserved for friends.
Just over the hill from Noblesville, past Riverview Hospital and down Cherrytree Avenue, is the house that Bill
built . . . or is building. It's not quite done, but Bill,
Nancy, and the boys moved in several months ago to
supervise those last finishing touches. The woodwork
isn't stained yet, the curtains haven't been hung, and
the new furniture is still on order. The Ashpaughs are
taking their time. They call this their dream house—a
large blue Cape Cod with dormer windows jutting over a
soon-to-be-seeded front yard, a pond out back with
horses nibbling at the green shoreline, and, of course, a
gym in the basement. You can't hurry dreams, they say.

Amid pounding hammers, Nancy sits in the kitchen at
a dinette table left over from their mobile home days. A
favorite Bill Ashpaugh story, please? She has several.
After all, they've been married ten years now. But she
chooses their first date, a special Wednesday evening
when Bill pulled up in front of her mother's house in a
battered old truck, wearing a gray electrician's uniform.
It wasn't that he was sloppy or didn't care enough to
dress up to take his new girl out for dinner, she later
learned. Actually, it was just the opposite. Too many
girls had sought Bill's company because he was a successful businessman and a prominent athlete. He
wanted Nancy to like him for himself, so he covered the
brawn with a uniform and left the sportscar at home.
They went to a nearby drive-in restaurant, munched
hamburgers, and talked for hours and hours. Several

weeks—and hamburgers—later, Bill invited her to attend the annual Mr. Indianapolis bodybuilding contest. When they arrived at Hofmeister's gym she was amazed to learn her date was not just a spectator, but the athlete favored to win first place over the other thirty competitors. She walked in with Bill, but she walked out three hours later with Mr. Indianapolis.

If everyone in Noblesville has a favorite Ashpaugh story, Bill is entitled to one, too. And his is *really* special. He tells it often, and gladly rearranges his work schedule so he can accommodate the many requests from groups that want to hear it. Whenever he stands in front of a microphone, the audience—no matter how young, tough, or street-wise—listens in total silence. Sometimes onlookers cry; but then, sometimes Bill cries too. The story is not selfish, and it doesn't concern trophies, titles, or cheering spectators. These things may still be a part of Bill's life, but they're not his primary motivation. No, this story deals with more important elements: a man who wouldn't die, a family that refused to give in, and a faith that challenged one of the most frightening enemies in America today and won.

Bill has told his story many times and now he's ready to tell it again. This time it stands alone, without benefit of any feat of strength for openers. No steel bar will be bent into a horseshoe, no telephone book will be ripped in half, and no hot-water bottle will be blown up until it bursts. These are the facts, recalled in Bill's own words. And if you're like most of the people around Noblesville, Indiana, after you read them, you'll have a favorite Bill Aspaugh story, too . . . one you'll remember for a long, long time.

Holly Miller
Anderson, Indiana

Chapter 1

NINETY-POUND WEAKLING

Shuffling along the side of a road, kicking a stone zig-zag style, first this way, then that, I must have looked as though I were held in place by two tall bookends—my big brothers—walking on either side of me. Dave, two years older, and Sam, three years my senior, were at least a head taller than I. But at age eight, I was the tough guy. Short and scrappy. What I lacked in muscle I more than made up in grit.

Walking the two-mile stretch from the family farm to downtown Westfield on Saturday afternoon was as much a part of the Ashpaugh kids' ritual as going to church on Sunday morning. Like most of the neighborhood short set, our goal was a little building behind the Shell station where free movies and cartoons were shown. But the real fun was the trek to town when my brothers challenged everyone along the way to take on little brother in a wrestling match.

Not that little brother minded. As soon as an opponent agreed to fight, I'd hand my popcorn money to Dave and roll up my sleeves. By the time the sleeves came down, I had usually been declared the winner and had proven once again I was king of the road. Sam would brush me off, patch me up, and tuck my shirttail back in place. With my popcorn money reinstated in my hip pocket, we'd continue the dusty pilgrimage to town—only this time the little guy in the middle felt as tall as the bookends. At least in my mind and in their eyes, I was Somebody. And when you're the youngest son in a family of three boys and three girls, that means a lot.

If winning roadside battles was my top priority in those days, keeping the victories secret was second on my list. When we'd finally arrive back at the farm late in the afternoon, Dave, the brains behind the brawn, would smuggle me upstairs to make me presentable for mom and dad. Scraped, burning knees were gently dabbed cool, and dust-brown hair was combed blond again. Somehow my parents never questioned why one of their boys always started the day squeaky clean and ended it looking like a street urchin with popped buttons, pocketless jeans, and a half-cup of sand in each shoe. But I don't think we fooled them for a minute.

As strict as they were about discipline, I think after much discussion they decided to look the other way when it came to my skirmishes. Just as Dave, Sam, and I plotted my wrestling matches from our bunks in the dorm-like room we shared upstairs, I think my folks decided behind closed doors in the master bedroom downstairs to let Bill develop his fighting spirit . . . in his own way.

They knew I was different from the other boys. For some reason, physical strength was more important to me. Hadn't I been the baby who had raised all six pounds of himself up on one arm just minutes after delivery? And hadn't I been the toddler who always had to jump higher, run faster, and throw farther than anyone else in the family? Maybe I never would make A-pluses like Dave and Sam. Maybe I was destined for something else. My parents might not have known just where I was going, but they were willing for me to find my own way—even if it meant an occasional skinned elbow, bruised shin, stubbed toe, or bloody nose.

I liked to let my fists do my talking for me. Anything was better than words as far as I was concerned. Because our family was so large and I was wedged between big brothers and little sisters, someone was always on hand to shelter me, answer for me, cover my shyness, and fill in for my shortcomings. If Bill were asked a question, Dave or Sam usually had the perfect reply. If they weren't available for comment, Shirley, Kay, and Lois constituted my back-up system. Such an in-house answering service was made to order.

I preferred to stay out of the spotlight, safely on the sidelines, surrounded and overshadowed by lots of noisy, happy family. I didn't want to be singled out or fussed over, or serve as the target for somebody's special attention.

When cousins, uncles, and aunts descended on the farm for one of mom's famous Sunday dinners, I dreaded the bear hugs and perfumed pecks on the cheeks that always began and ended the get-togethers. As soon as the huggers and kissers moved past me to focus their attention on the little Ashpaughs—first Kay and then Lois Anne—I'd make my escape to the barn, where I'd burrow into the hay mound and fantasize about being the biggest and strongest boy ever to come out of Westfield Elementary.

I had a long way to go. Not only was I the smallest first-grader in school, I was also the youngest. With an October 6th birthday, somehow I managed to squeak in under the deadline and qualify as class runt. Though I dreamed of being Superman, I came closer to resembling a pint-sized version of Clark Kent, complete with glasses, hair "Brylcreem-ed" into a soft Dairy Queen swirl, and a jaw clamped shut in silent resolve. I was the short, silent type. But oh, I had dreams!

Mickey Mantle was ranking hero in those days and I was as big a fan of the walloping switch-hitter as I could be under the circumstances. Television didn't invade the Ashpaugh premises until I was in high school, so all news of the awesome Yankees and their star center fielder had to come from the old console radio in the living room. Not that it mattered. My day started at dawn with milking duties, then it was on to school, and finally more farm chores at night. Such a schedule left little time to follow the triumphs of the Bronx Bombers.

The stories mom and dad read to us before bedtime each night provided more immediate heroes. It was a tradition around home that no matter how tired we were, we'd settle down for an hour of devotions before dad declared lights out. The youngest offspring—and that changed often—was given the place of honor on mom's lap, and the rest of us fanned out on the sofa and spilled over onto the floor. Except for occasional pokes, fidgets, and pinches in the ribs, we'd listen intently to the evening's Scripture lesson. When the chapter was marked and the Bible closed for another night, mom would give the signal for the appointed song leader to end the makeshift vesper service on a happy, though decidedly off-key, note. What we lacked in talent we made up for in volume. The Osmonds of Utah had nothing to fear from the Ashpaughs of Indiana!

My favorite biblical heroes were the strong men. I never grew tired of hearing the stories of David and Goliath or Samson. I not only wanted to learn about them, I wanted to *be* like them. Although they were of a different era and had lived halfway around the world from Indiana, I could relate to them from my perch on a Hoosier hay mound more easily than I could identify with more contemporary superstars. The biblical giants were quiet, like me, but their muscle said what their voices couldn't. So would mine.

Somewhere along the line I became convinced that to be strong—really strong—a man must never show his emotions. And that held for boys, too. Tears were forbidden, according to my philosophy, and I refused to let anyone see me cry. It wasn't easy. Mom tells me that as a baby, I rolled off the sofa onto the hardwood floor and bumped my head. She cried, but I didn't.

Years later I remember taking a spill from the back of a cow I was riding during a backyard rodeo performance staged for the benefit of the neighborhood gang. While I was acting the part of bronco-buster, one of our "spectators" crept up behind me and whacked the cow on the flank. I sailed across the back forty in a perfect arc and came in for a crash landing on my elbow. Ouch! Somehow I managed to stumble to the house and was halfway up the stairs in search of "medic" Dave when Mom stopped me.

"What's the matter, Bill?" she asked.

"Nothing," I answered in my usual talkative manner.

"I know there's something wrong. You're as white as a sheet," she said, reaching for the mangled arm. She was right, of course—mothers almost always are—and within two hours the broken bone was set, torn flesh stitched, and a protective splint carefully bound in place. All this was accomplished without my shedding a single tear.

If strong men don't cry, neither do they shirk a challenge. And if you happened to have been unlucky enough to be a follower of Bill Ashpaugh in the 1950s, you adhered to his example. As a kid, about the only follower I could lure into the fold was my baby sister, Lois Anne, six years my junior. Sometimes I look at her today, a slim, pretty mother of two with an active ministry of her own, and I honestly wonder how she survived the hair-raising stunts I put her through.

When she was three years old, I decided it was high time she learned to swim, so I tossed her in the seven-foot-deep creek and told her to sink or paddle. Luckily for both of us, she chose the latter and floundered to shore, but it was the last time she went near the water until she was a teenager. She had barely recovered from that trauma when I realized I had neglected to teach her the fine points of riding a bicycle. This was easily remedied by putting her on mine and heading her down the hill with a bellowing command to "Ride!" Under the circumstances, that's all she *could* do.

During my sandlot baseball career, I recruited Lois Anne to field the fly balls that I usually smashed in the direction of the tomato patch or corn rows. Mom always kept her babies in white high-top shoes until they started school, and I can still see Lois chasing my line drives into the garden with her white leather shoes glistening in the sun, only to emerge minutes later ankle-deep in mud, but grinning because she had retrieved the ball.

One year, after hanging up the cleats and glove for another season, I decided to pursue a circus career (rodeos were *verboten* since my elbow escapade) and turned to my half-pint sidekick for support. Lois Anne wasn't sure she was ready to run away and join the Big Top until I convinced her of the vital role she was to play in my act. After all, who else could I get to hold a piece of paper between her teeth while I attempted to crack it out of her mouth with a twelve-foot bullwhip?

Don't get the idea that my childhood mission in life was to destroy my baby sister. I was as devoted to her as she was to me. We all were. Each morning as we traipsed past her room on the way outside to do our before-school chores we'd stop, one at a time, to plant a wet kiss on her cheek. Then in the evening we'd tiptoe past her crib, look both ways for disapproving adults, then sneak in for a grimy good-night smooch on the forehead.

She was the self-proclaimed family pacifier. When dad was forced to resort to his peachtree discipline— we never got more than one or two gentle swipes with the branch—Lois Anne would plead with mom for a reprieve. When she felt the family unity was threatened by big sister Shirley's pending marriage plans, she decided to maintain the status quo by removing Shirley's engagement ring from the dresser and hiding it in the stove. Her reasoning was simple: How could a girl possibly get married without a ring? (No, it didn't work.) After mom had declared an edict that we kids could bring home no more stray dogs and cats, and I came over the hill carrying a baby billy goat, it was Lois Anne who pointed out, "But mom, it's not a dog or a cat."

I probably felt closest to my little sister, not because of the abuse she willingly let me bestow on her, but because she accepted me without question. She never minded that I was shy, a little quieter than the rest of the clan, and a little more awkward. When I'd creep off to cry silent tears in the hayloft or high up in a tree, she'd post herself as guard and protect my need for privacy. All at a discreet distance, of course.

School was particularly painful for me. I was so bashful that I'd cower behind the girl seated in front of me rather than risk the teacher spotting me and asking me to read aloud. I'd try to concoct new excuses every day as to why I couldn't possibly recite this poem or that chapter in front of my classmates. Laryngitis. Sore throat. Hay fever. The teacher must have thought I was not only the youngest and smallest guy in school, but also the sickliest. Or, maybe not. Maybe I didn't convince her of my persistent voice problems any more than I fooled mom and dad about my roadside wrestling matches on those Saturday afternoons.

It always came back to fighting. I couldn't find the nerve to sign up for debate team or speech class, but I didn't have any trouble winning wordless matches on the playground. As much as I loved music, I never could bring myself to join the church choir—I was convinced one look at the congregation would silence me for life—yet I could challenge the biggest guy in Sunday School to a battle after the service. At the junior-senior play I offered to pull the curtain rather than take an onstage speaking role, but it didn't faze me to pass time between acts in arm-wrestling contests with half the football team. In a two-against-one match I was always the "one" and I was usually the winner.

Our school's athletic program was limited. For light-weights like myself, participation was a matter of choice: basketball or baseball. Football was strictly a spectator sport unless you were tall and muscular. I was neither. Although I was undoubtedly the strongest guy at Westfield High, I wasn't given the option of developing my potential. In those days, coaches shied away from building athletes. You were either born that way or you joined the band. Lifting weights and following such carefully prescribed exercise programs as we see today were unheard of. Physical education teachers warned of students' becoming "muscle-bound," whatever that meant. Minor sports—boxing, wrestling, tennis, and golf—were either ignored because of budgetary dictates, or they were offered only on a limited basis. If you weren't built like Hercules, you might as well resign yourself to earning your school letter on the cheering squad.

Any aspirations I had for an athletic career were further thwarted by the no-sports position of our small country church. Dedicated church members, my parents let us follow our inclinations though it meant they bore the church leaders' criticism concerning our participation in sports, Boy Scouts, and 4-H. Once, when Dave and I attended services in our Scout uniforms, we were the topic of the extemporaneous sermon. We might have squirmed a little out of sheer embarrassment. But, taking our cue from mom and dad, we endured the disapproving glares and sat straight and tall.

What I didn't realize during my early high school years was that I was on the most stringent training program possible for a boy my age. No coach could have put me through more rigorous paces if he had sat down and plotted it out on paper. The key factor was work—hard farm labor.

It all began the summer I was twelve, when I took my first paying job as a hay baler. Our family was lucky. With six little ones of assorted sizes and temperaments, we had a built-in work force. Some nearby farmers weren't so fortunate and were more than happy to hire one or two or three of the sturdy Ashpaugh boys to pitch in and help out. We were used to it.

As soon as we were able to toddle around after mom in our white high-tops, we were expected to lend a hand in our truck garden. The corn, tomatoes, squash, and other produce we grew were a means of underwriting the "extras" that dad's job in Naval avionics couldn't always provide.

Those of us who weren't weeding, watering, and harvesting the vegetables were out on the highway supervising the sales end of our thriving roadside business. The girls were especially good at this, knowing that every addition to the family coffers would bolster the back-to-school wardrobe fund or pay admission to the State Fair in August. The boys thought in terms of new bicycles or new catcher's mitts, while the little Ashpaughs were concerned with racing from garden to highway, keeping the family vegetable "market" well stocked with fresh-off-the-vine produce. Theirs was piecework—one tomato, two ears of corn, a single zucchini at a time. The work kept everyone occupied, and shortly after dark we were more than willing to collapse in our beds.

Once I began hiring out as a hay baler, I started hoarding my money, tucking it away in my bureau drawer and spending my spare time dreaming about what I would buy. The temptations were few, since our rural area afforded no movie theaters (the Saturday afternoon free "film festival" behind the Shell station didn't really count) or toy stores within walking distance to lure us into spending the hard-earned nest egg.

Summer days passed quickly . . . up at dawn, big breakfast, out in the fields early to pitch great forkfuls of hay into high yellow domes. By the time I was fifteen, my work uniform included a white sailor's hat, thanks to Sam, recently recruited by the U.S. Navy. I was so proud of that hat that I wouldn't take it off long enough for mom to wash it.

Working under the scorching Hoosier sun, I became browner, blonder, and stronger every week, every season. Even the veteran farmhands admitted that no one could bale hay in a higher pile than I. To most kids, such a compliment would be shrugged off as unimportant. But to me, the bashful little guy who never could make the football team, it was just what I needed to hear. The words reinforced my goal—the same goal I had nurtured since the days of skinned knees, bruised shins, and roadside wrestling matches. I wanted to be bigger, stronger, and tougher than anyone else in Indiana. But how?

Like every other kid growing up in America in the 50s, I dawdled over the Charles Atlas advertisements in the back of the comic books we furtively exchanged at school. I read the promises over and over, flexed my all-but-non-existent biceps and read some more. The success stories seemed a little silly, even to an un-sophisticated teenager like myself, and after several years of farm work, I was hardly the duplicate of the scrawny guy who spent his summers getting sand kicked in his face. *Still, maybe a set of weights could help me develop the muscles that were starting to sprout under my shirt,* I thought. *Okay, okay,* I decided, *what do I have to lose besides my entire life's savings?* Dilemma resolved, one memorable morning I reached into the far corner of my bureau drawer, counted my cache one last time, and sat down to fill out the order blank that was guaranteed to bring me fame, fortune, and maybe a date to the junior-senior prom.

Chapter 2

SUCCESS: GROWING UP
AND UP AND UP

One month. Four weeks. Thirty days. I studied the calendar tacked up on the kitchen bulletin board and counted. But the result was always the same—the box wouldn't arrive until the end of September. I felt like the little boy in *The Music Man* who waits for his band instrument to be delivered by way of a jostling Wells Fargo wagon. But my weights were coming via Railway Express, all the way from Pennsylvania, and would not be tossed from a stagecoach onto bustling Main Street in River City, Iowa. Instead, they would be transported from the downtown depot in a belching, snorting truck to a steamy one-room gym somewhere on Ohio Street in Indianapolis.

The price tag read $38, so I knew they had to be special—the best, in fact—since that mind-boggling total represented countless days of pitching hay high into the back of a baler. After all, even an experienced farmhand like myself only commanded an hourly wage of sixty cents.

I passed the weeks dreaming about what the weights would look like, how quickly I'd see evidence of their magic, how soon it would be before the kids at school would notice the "new" Bill Ashpaugh. The rest of the family was only mildly interested in my investment, and mom silently labeled it a new trend, just another phase in Bill's growing process, much the same as horses, baseball, and my short-lived career as a circus daredevil.

Still, there were rules, carefully laid down in advance by mom and dad and grudgingly agreed to by me: Under no circumstances were the weights ever to find their way into the house. The dilapidated chicken coop out back would have to double as a makeshift gym. Okay? *Okay.* Also, under no circumstances could lifting weights interfere with the more important aspects of Ashpaugh family life—chores, church, and, ugh, homework. All right? *Hmmm, I guess so.*

When the Big Day finally arrived, I was prepared. I had arranged in advance for a friend with a driver's license to drive me the twenty-five miles south to pick up my very special delivery. In return, he was assured *carte blanche* use of my chicken coop with all its sophisticated physical fitness equipment. Each of us felt he had struck the better bargain at the other's expense, and we chattered all the way to Indianapolis about the rigid training schedule we planned to initiate that very afternoon.

We circled the block three times before we spotted the sign for the gym, shoved in a second-story window of an old office building. Up a flight of stairs and down a narrow, dark hall we found our destination . . . a small, dingy room with a decidedly unpleasant smell about it. For a minute, I questioned the wisdom of my purchase.

Then I looked, really looked, and saw all I had ever fantasized, jammed into one compact, shabby little area. Did I say shabby? No, it was wonderful. Barbells of various sizes and weights were lined up on support tracks. Punching bags swung lazily from S-hooks in the ceiling. And a medicine ball slouched like a round sausage bursting its casing in the corner. The smell . . . what smell? . . . suddenly seemed inoffensive and natural.

When I recovered from the wonder of the hardware, I noticed what probably was the most magnificent sight in the entire room. It was not mechanical, but human. Standing six-foot-four and weighing in excess of two hundred pounds, his body glistened with perspiration as he carefully heaved over his head an enormous bar laden with several iron discs. Mr. Higgins, owner of the gym, recognized the awe in my eyes and guided me over to the weight lifter for a personal audience.

"Bill, meet Peter Lupus," he said, gently shoving me in the direction of the body beautiful. Thank goodness, I didn't know at the time that Lupus was destined not only to win the Mr. Indiana bodybuilding title, but to one day be a regular on the *Mission Impossible* television series and a successful film actor. As it was, I eagerly put out my hand for a hearty wrenching. Later, I would learn that Lupus wasn't the only celebrity in the gym. Mr. Higgins, the kindly owner who took me under his wing that day, had won a few honors himself—including an Olympic medal in weight lifting.

With help from my new acquaintances, the precious box—all 110 pounds of it—was loaded, unopened, into our car and transported back to Westfield. From there it was shuttled to the coop which I already had mentally transformed into a carbon copy of Higgins' gym.

But Mr. Higgins never would have sanctioned the meager equipment I discovered when I finally tore open the box. Buried in the mounds of shredded newspaper was a single set of dumbbells. I dug my hands down through the packing in search of a bar. No luck. The sum total of my sophisticated set of weights, guaranteed to strengthen the pectorals, trim the torso, and build the biceps, could be held in two hands. I didn't need a chicken coop to house my gym . . . a shoebox would do nicely.

If my vision hadn't been expanded by the visit to the gym—the *real* gym—I might have tried to recoup my thirty-eight-dollar loss by demanding a refund. But I couldn't let go of the dream, especially now that I knew it was attainable. Hadn't I seen Peter Lupus? Didn't I know now what was possible with the right kind of training and the correct type of discipline? I opened the pamphlet that accompanied my "equipment" and began to study it, stopping frequently to flex, curl, squat, and lift. If I learned one thing during that first workout, it was that I had a long, long way to go.

I decided to establish a routine, a strictly defined regimen, and stick to it. Remembering my promise to mom that my weight lifting wouldn't interfere with church, chores, and school, I had to find a couple of hours in the day's schedule to shoehorn in a regular workout.

Evenings were impossible because dad needed me to help with the endless remodeling of the farm. He was a do-it-yourself buff and I was his right hand, or rather his left hand, since I'm a southpaw. Daytime hours were booked with school nine months of the year and farm work in the summer. That left only the early morning, beginning at 5:30 A.M., when mom was hovering over the stove brewing the day's first pot of coffee, dad was shaving in the bathroom right off the kitchen, and the junior Ashpaughs were snugly tucked in their beds upstairs.

I can still remember my parents shaking their heads in unison as I plodded through the kitchen half-awake, stumbled out the back door and down to the chicken coop. I knew they were patiently waiting for this "phase" to run its course. But autumn turned to winter, and winter blossomed into spring, and the distance between the house and coop was still linked by a well-worn path of red Indiana clay. This was one stage I had no intention of outgrowing.

At first, my gym was filled to overflowing with friends and family. Dave would duck in long enough to say hi, and huff and puff his way through an abbreviated warm-up routine. Guys from school would stop by to work up a sweat before moving on to more pressing and entertaining pastimes.

But the glamour of the neighborhood gym quickly wore thin, and visitors were less and less frequent. I was the only regular customer, encouraged by an ever-increasing library of weight lifting books and here's-how-you-do-it brochures and buoyed by words of support from my favorite little cheerleader in residence, Lois Anne.

The early morning sessions were spent in total solitude with nothing to amuse me but my thoughts. As my body went through its now-familiar paces, my brain chewed on the same dreams and aspirations I had fed it as a child. I was going to be the biggest, strongest, most muscular man in Westfield, or maybe in the whole state of Indiana. I was beginning to think any goal was attainable for the person who wanted it badly enough and was willing to work hard for it. I was willing, and oh, how badly I wanted it. Of one thing I was certain: No one ever hears about the guy who quits. I was determined never to give up.

My world expanded by several miles when I turned sixteen and became the proud owner of a 1946 Ford coupe, complete with a souped-up Mercury engine. Mom chalked it up to yet another phase. My talent as a budding wheeler-dealer surfaced when I traded a .30-.30 caliber rifle and an old radio for a 1929 Model A roadster. Not realizing its potential value, I proceeded to lower it, chop it up, and install an Oldsmobile engine in it.

When the tinkering-with-antique-cars phase finally wore off, I was left with a mound of mismatched fenders, an assortment of running boards, an array of oddly shaped headlamps and one natty little rumble seat.

Bowing to dad's ultimatum, I gave it all away to a neighbor who dabbled in "junque." "So much for *that* stage," my parents sighed with relief, but my fascination with weight lifting held fast.

With the addition of wheels to my life, I was able to look beyond the adjoining farms for possible employment. Anyone familiar with Westfield—and there aren't many of us—knows its proximity to the many prosperous cities and towns in Central Indiana: Noblesville to the East, Carmel to the South, Cicero to the North, and Lebanon to the West. Hardly giant metropolises, but still, each little burg boasted a thriving business or two.

Studying my daily schedule, I decided if dad could spare me from remodeling duties, I might be able to work second shift, from 3 P.M. to midnight, at a local factory. Such a job would leave little time for homework, but that was one obligation I had never lost sleep over. I began making the rounds of personnel offices, filling out endless application forms, and learning more about the jobs I wasn't qualified to do than about the few I could handle with ease.

"Can you type?" I was asked by a middle-aged spinster who looked a little like "Our Miss Brooks."

"No," I replied honestly.

"How are your bookkeeping skills?"

"Huh?"

"Ever run a drill press?" she queried, trying a different tack.

"Sorry."

So was she. I made a mental note to try a little harder and listen a little more closely to my teachers in the future. Maybe school wasn't such a waste of time, after all. Bill Ashpaugh was definitely beginning to grow up—and it was about time.

Success is often reached in strange places. Mine was lurking in a cotton candy factory on the rural outskirts of

Arcadia, about a twenty-minute drive from the farm. Yes, the foreman assured me, he was hiring. And yes, I responded gleefully, I could start the next afternoon. But my euophoria was short-lived. Take it from me— working among chocolate nougat, salt water taffy, and jawbreakers might sound like the answer to every boy's dream, but it has its drawbacks. I don't care what Willie Wonka says.

My first on-the-job assignment was to clean the enormous machines that oozed chocolate like our giant maple trees out back bled thick, slow-moving syrup. A scrape here, a taste there. The chocolate was rich and sweet and our wages weren't garnisheed for occasional samples. What more could a guy ask for—right? Wrong. At first it was all delicious, then it was merely good, and finally it was unbearable. After exactly one week I was totally immune to temptation.

Even today, when a great home-cooked meal is topped off with a gooey dessert, I almost always decline. People marvel at my extraordinary willpower, but I can't take any credit. I trace my ability to abstain to the two long years when I divided my time and talents between stirring great copper kettlefuls of peanut brittle and supervising the manufacture of nut clusters. Moderation is the key to all of life's delicacies, and speaking as one who once overdosed at the Arcadia Cotton Candy Company, mine is the voice of experience.

Life began to change at home as the Ashpaugh chicks spread their wings and the nest began to empty. Despite Lois Anne's ingenious plot to cancel Shirley's wedding by hiding her diamond engagement ring in the stove, our big sister soon was happily married and planning a family of her own. Sam was off in the Navy and Dave was serving an apprenticeship at a nearby electrical company.

Thanks to a recommendation by Dave to his employer, I landed a summer job as an electrician's assistant and was rescued forever from a life of peanut clusters and chronic acne. Maybe Dave was trying to make amends for all those fights he had arranged for me back in my preschool days. Or, maybe he was just getting tired of receiving peanut brittle every birthday, Christmas, and Easter.

The farm underwent a facelift too. Dad's remodeling efforts became more obvious as the offspring grew up and moved out. No longer were there six pairs of little hands to slow his progress. A glassed-in porch was added out back so mom could do her ironing in the bright morning sunlight and line the window sills with starts of tomato and summer squash plants for next season's garden. New, white aluminum siding covered old decaying clapboard on the outside, and dark green carpet made hardwood floors warm to the toes on the inside.

Although my job and training schedules left little time for extra projects, I enjoyed working alongside dad as he turned a no-frills farmhouse into a comfortable, and in some ways, luxurious home. I loved the idea of taking basic, raw materials and turning them into solid, tangible tools of living. Such skills seemed so practical and real compared to the subject matter stressed in the classroom. To this day, I've never lost my enthusiasm for creating something from nothing, especially when that "something" makes my family's life a little easier and a lot more comfortable.

This preoccupation with building eventually would expand into a full-time profession, although I didn't realize it at the time. Just as baling hay was training me for my favorite avocation, dad's patient lessons in planning, measuring, sawing, and pounding were preparing me for my life's work.

School was still at the bottom of my list of priorities,

and I'm not sure who was more relieved—my parents, my teachers, or myself—when graduation was imminent. The Ashpaugh honor roll tradition, so firmly established by Shirley, Kay, and Dave, came to a grinding halt when I donned a black cap and gown and solemnly joined my thirty-one classmates in the step-hesitation-step processional across the familiar gym floor. But first came senior week—a breathless series of activities guaranteed to leave participants exhausted and pliant as they awaited their next challenge in life, whether it be marriage, work, or college.

I had grown up a lot in my four years at Westfield High School, but I wasn't done yet. I was still shy and preferred the sidelines to the forefront, and was more suited to the role of follower than leader. No longer class runt, somewhere during the years when no one was looking—or at least noticing me—I had shot up to a lanky six feet. But I was all hands and feet. If someone had put a pair of white cotton gloves on me, I might have doubled as Jiminy Cricket.

A latecomer to Westfield "society," I dated only when necessary. If a senior party specified couples only, I would wait until the last possible moment, gulp three deep breaths of air for luck (and to ensure my voice wouldn't crack), call an underclassmate and issue a terse-and-to-the-point invitation. Younger girls weren't nearly as terrifying as "older women," and besides, they were more likely to accept my nervous offer.

I was far more comfortable in the company of the guys—riding horses, lifting weights, or drag racing through town—much to the dismay of my parents and the town marshal. I'd do anything on a dare and seldom lost. Most challenges were easy, especially those involving strength, endurance, or speed.

Others were almost impossible. Imagine shy, bashful Bill Ashpaugh with hair slicked back in a wet ducktail doing an imitation of Elvis Presley at senior skits night. I was awful. The hips circled in an awkward bump and grind; the mouth opened, but nothing came out. *Wait a minute,* I thought, *this isn't the way we rehearsed it.* I was supposed to be pantomiming a record. I shot an I'll-get-you-for-this glare at my "assistant" backstage and he retaliated with a grin. I clenched my fists as a reminder that I was Bill, not Elvis, and I possessed Hamilton County's most fabled left hook. He wilted. The record revved up and the familiar sounds of "You Ain't Nothing But A Hound Dog" blasted forth. Whew! I synchronized my mouth to the words and silently dedicated the last line to my buddy in the wings. At that point, he certainly was no friend of mine.

The final event of our senior year was to be the highlight of our high school careers. Two buses were chartered to transport the thirty-two proud graduates plus teachers plus parent chaperones to Gettysburg, Washington, D.C., and New York City. Most of us had never been farther east than the Ohio state line. This was the big time, the real thing, but it carried a price tag and I was expected to pay my own share.

Being the entrepreneur that I was, all my "funds" were tied up in merchandise: fenders, running boards, a rumble seat, and my weights. I assessed the situation and decided to liquidate. The market for mismatched auto parts didn't look too promising, so, after wavering first in one direction and then the other, I put the word out on the street that Ashpaugh's chicken coop was having a clearance sale.

Before I could change my mind, a scrawny little guy who reminded me a little bit of Clark Kent and a lot of myself, presented himself at the "gym" door with an envelope of cash he had saved from his job as a summer farmhand. He made me an offer I couldn't refuse. Hmmm, isn't this where I came in?

Chapter 3

THE GYM: A ROOM FOR IMPROVEMENT

"We're going to take Ashpaugh to New York City and leave him there," joked our class sponsor as we boarded the buses, cranked open the windows, and hung halfway out to wave jubilant goodbyes to sleepy-eyed parents. They returned the gesture like wind-up dolls that are winding down. Even at 6 A.M., the school's parking lot was hazy with heat and the day promised to be what mom always called "a real scorcher."

The class trip was the final indulgence of careless-ness, the last gasp of collective fun before we became individuals again. A handful of students would be given a reprieve in the fall when they would head for West Lafayette and Purdue University to remain "kids" for another four years.

Most of us would be shoved into instant adulthood within two weeks. Jobs were waiting. Or weddings. For some, the heavy responsibility of parenting was only a year or two away. Somehow, the wheezing, pungent buses that were to transport us from Indiana to New York were also to convey us from one phase of our lives to the next. We were to leave as students and return as adults. The transition would be made sometime within the ten days away from home. Somewhere along Highway 40.

The class trip wasn't as important to me as it was to

some of my classmates. I viewed high school graduation as a beginning rather than an end. I was a late
bloomer, just coming into my own, just starting to gain
confidence and feel good about myself.

I had been offered an apprenticeship at the same
electrical company whre Dave worked, and the job
promised a steady income, an opportunity to learn, and
the security of a lifetime profession once I earned my
master electrician's license.

I was excited at the prospect of becoming an adult.
After ten days of *oohing* and *aahing* at monuments and
skyscrapers, when the bus doors finally folded open to
spill a new crop of grownups onto the blacktop parking
lot behind Westfield High School, I was the first one off.
I knew where I was going and I was more excited about
the trip ahead than the one we had just completed.
School had been fun. Washington, D.C., New York City,
and Gettysburg were great. But I was looking forward to
something even better (whatever it might be!).

First order of business was to refurbish the "gym."
But this time I wouldn't be satisfied with a lone set of
dumbbells. I wanted more, and with a forty-hour
paycheck issued promptly at 5 P.M. every Friday, I could
afford the luxury. Luxury? Hardly. For me it was a neces-
sity.

A few friends, at loose ends after high school graduation, decided to join in the physical fitness effort. We
laid claim to a two-car garage and began furnishing it
with wall-to-wall weights, bars, a power rack, and a
small rowing machine. Remembering my old chicken
coop days, I knew a regular training schedule was es-
sential. So I set aside two or three hours every evening
before dinner—but it wasn't enough. A weekend
round-the-clock drive to York, Pennsylvania, for my first
look at an organized weight lifting competition convinced me of that. What bodies! What discipline!

If I were to really learn this sport, I knew I needed to train with guys who were better than I. At our little garage-gym I was the best, and that just wasn't good enough. I thought back to the first gym I had ever seen—the dingy room in Indianapolis—where at age fifteen I had met Peter Lupus. Was it still there? Was *he* still there? Did I have the nerve to walk in again, this time as "one of the boys"?

I gathered together five would-be weight lifters from Westfield and talked them into carpooling the twenty-five miles south to the Olympic Health Club on Ohio Street. They had been the football heroes at Westfield High, the Mr. Machos, the guys who were used to performing to an audience.

After a few weeks, when they learned no squad of cheerleaders was turning cartwheels and no bleacher-fuls of fans were yelling us on, they lost interest, dropped off, and quit. One by one, each found a reason why he couldn't possibly make the trip every day to heave, sweat, and push his body to the point of near-exhaustion. I didn't blame them, but neither did I share their lack of interest. Everything they objected to, I rejoiced in.

"Too hot," they complained.

"Invigorating!" I responded.

"Too tiring."

"Rejuvenating!" I countered.

"Too far."

"Twenty minutes if you hit the traffic lights right."

Gradually new friends replaced the old and Peter Lupus—my hero for four years—made a place for me in his corner of the gym. He was training for the Mr. Indiana contest and all his energies were directed toward his quest for the title. He sold cars to underwrite his expenses, which he kept to the barest minimum.

All luxuries were eliminated, and that included laundry. Pete had the grubbiest sweat clothes in the gym and the rest of us took bets on whether or not they could stand up on their own. Actually, I think if he had looked the other way they might have walked out the door without him.

All the sacrifices proved worthwhile the night he finally won the state's top bodybuilding honor. I was in the audience cheering him on, along with half the female population of Indianapolis. A guy might give up laundry, but girls were something else. Priorities, you know.

Watching Peter being photographed with an enormous silver trophy that resembled a multi-tiered wedding cake, complete with swags, columns, and statuary, underscored the single bit of philosophy I had carried with me so many years: Nobody remembers the guy who quits. Peter Lupus never gave up and now he, his trophy, and a Hollywood agent were heading West to see if anyone cared. They did. The next time I saw him was on television. What he had accomplished would become my goal too, I decided.

But before I could consider any Lupus-like competition for myself, I needed to learn about the different types of weight lifting and decide what I liked best and in which area I had the most potential.

Just as there are various kinds of "ball"—football, baseball, basketball, soccer—so is there a variety of weight lifting categories. No one is simply a weight lifter; nor is anyone merely a ballplayer. I learned that three separate divisions are clustered loosely under the umbrella term of weight lifting: Olympic lifting, powerlifting, and physique (also called bodybuilding).

From my vantage point in the gym, I could watch specialists in each area honing their skills and directing their talents toward their chosen goals. I listened as coaches guided athletes through carefully planned programs to correct weaknesses and build strength, form, and confidence. I heard the tips, advice, and complaints exchanged between teachers and students, masters and novices. I tucked them away for future reference. Like a squirrel I hoarded the bits of wisdom until the day when I might benefit from them—until that far-off time when the sophisticated and advanced guidelines of competition might apply to me.

But first I had to decide which area of lifting I wanted to claim as my own. I was no longer the backyard generalist who dabbled in weights when he wasn't supervising a kettle of peanut brittle, hitting line drives into the back forty, or terrorizing the town marshal by peeling through Westfield in a mufflerless coupe. It was time to get serious.

Powerlifting, I learned, is the sport of the superstrong. Pure, primitive, easy to understand—it's sheer strength, with little emphasis on technique or appearance. A powerlift competition requires participants to vie with one another in three different lifts—the *squat,* the *bench press,* and the *deadlift.* The number of pounds lifted in the three events are added together for the athlete's score, with the highest number deciding the winner. For spectators, powerlifting is exciting in its simplicity. The best athlete is easily identified by his brute strength with no nebulous factors such as form, technique, and style entering into the judges' decision. The winner is the guy or gal who lifts the most weight in the *squat*—where the competitor begins in a standing position with the bar across the shoulders, does a deep knee bend and returns to an upright stance with his knees locked; or the *bench press*—where he lies on his back with the bar lowered over his chest and pushes it upward until the arms are straight; or the *deadlift*—where the bar is laid in front of the lifter's feet, gripped with both hands and lifted until the competitor is standing with knees locked and shoulders thrust back.

Although I respected the purity of the sport and the enormous dedication of its participants, powerlifting didn't hold the fascination for me that Olympic lifting did. Whereas Olympic lifting is a two-lift competition, more emphasis is placed on balance, flexibility, and coordination. It is the sport of that phenomenal 345-pound Russian superheavyweight, Vasily Alexeev, who has proven he can outlift the rest of the world.

Fortunately for us less robust athletes, competition is divided into weight classes, beginning at 114½ pounds, progressing to 123½, 132¼, 148¾, and upwards to the heaviest category, over 242½ pounds. To the connoisseur, the two lifts—the *snatch* and the *clean and jerk*—can be as beautiful as a well-executed axel or "Hamill camel" is to a figure skating buff.

When the lifter pulls the weight from the floor and raises it straight over his head in one, unbroken motion (the *snatch*), spectators and judges evaluate the total performance. When the athlete lifts the weight from the floor to his chest in one motion, then raises it overhead in another movement (the *clean and jerk*), attention is paid to technique and coordination as well as to strength. The extra challenge of maintaining balance and developing flexibility intrigued me. It wasn't that I felt Olympic lifting was a better sport than powerlifting. It merely seemed better suited to my interests and skills.

Never a serious option was bodybuilding, which I viewed as a sissy sport. The idea of pouring myself into a pair of skimpy trunks, splashing on baby oil, and flexing my muscles under a posing light for the benefit of seven judges and a roomful of screaming fans turned me off completely. I had attended physique contests, seen guys herded across the stage like a parade of numbered cattle, and watched them tense first this muscle then that, while a panel of critics sat in review.

Leave the cheesecake to the girls in Atlantic City, I thought. Give me a real he-man's sport.

What I didn't realize was that the bodybuilder is often the strongest guy in the gym. A weight lifter must execute a certain lift only once to win, but the bodybuilder pumps iron constantly in order to build up the muscles it takes to come out on top. Because of this rigorous training regimen, he usually has more endurance and stamina than the powerlifter and Olympic lifter combined. To the lifter, weights are the end; to the bodybuilder, weights are the means to the end. The trophy doesn't go to the man who lifts the most weight, but to the guy who has the best developed body—a body shaped, molded, and chiseled by lifting weights.

For some reason, at the age of twenty, I didn't appreciate the uniqueness of the part-sport, part-spectacle phenomenon called bodybuilding. Participants were merely pretty boys, as far as I was concerned—paper tigers who spent most of their time flexing in front of great banks of mirrors, posing to music, shaving the hair off their bodies and rubbing quick tanning cream on their skin when the weather wasn't right for basking in the sun. Ugh!

Once established as an Olympic weight-lifter-in-training, I began exercising every other day for about three or four hours after work. This, I learned, was better than those daybreak workouts of my chicken coop years. By 5 P.M. my body was warmed up from eight hours on the job, but I wasn't yet exhausted. Since I was told never to exercise on either a full or empty stomach, I established the habit of stopping by a local watering hole for something light—a salad, juice, or a little high-protein tuna—before heading for the gym.

My training schedule was carefully monitored by several of the "pros," and consisted of exercises grouped into sets. A series of lifts repeated a certain number of times (repetitions) makes up one set. A short rest is usually taken before the next set is begun. The initial set of a workout is the easiest, with each subsequent series becoming progressively harder. I might start out lifting 135 pounds five times, then lift 165 pounds three times, then 175 pounds three times, then onward and upward. With each outpouring of energy, the blood vessels in the muscles fill up with fresh, oxygen-laden blood. The muscles expand or "pump up" and the athlete feels invigorated and powerful. Although the spurt of expansion is temporary, the healthy feeling endures long after the workout, and the muscle-building process continues.

Just as my body benefited from my new weight lifting program, so did my self-confidence. Call me old-fashioned, but I believe it's man's instinct to want to be strong. It's ingrained in us, and any man who denies it isn't telling the whole truth. Think about it: What woman doesn't want to be pretty? And what man doesn't want to be strong?

When people finally noticed the emergence of the "new" Bill Ashpaugh, I felt the first stirrings of pride and self-worth. As I began to fill out my shirts, guys at work wanted to know what I was doing. Could they do it too? I was growing bigger and bigger in their eyes—and in mine. I was somebody. Really somebody.

All my thoughts and energies were targeted toward my goal of physical perfection. I was totally absorbed with myself—how I looked, how I felt, and how I appeared to the rest of the world. I easily recognized my physical shortcomings and admitted there was room for improvement. But my preoccupation with "self" ended there. I never considered my spiritual well-being might benefit from some attention and nurturing too. My total dedication to my appearance crowded out any thoughts of God's stake in all this activity. There would be time for

Him later, I assured myself. As for now—first things first.

Not all the credit for the new me could be attributed to the huff-and-puff rigors of lifting weights. The atmosphere in the gym was as conducive to growth as the controlled, positive environment of a greenhouse. Everyone present had the same goals—to better himself, to grow stronger and healthier, and to look and feel better.

The gym is a great equalizer. With everyone wearing old sweat clothes, no one knows or cares who has money, power, or position. The guy to my right may be a bank president, while the man next to him may be on parole from the state prison. I might train with an athlete for six months and never know he's a Baptist preacher, a doctor, or a janitor . . . we're too busy talking shop . . . weights and measures, you know. Not until we shower, get back into the "uniforms" of our trade—a pinstripe suit for the banker, jeans for the parolee, a dark suit for the preacher, and coveralls for me—do the differences in our life styles and social stations surface. By then we like each other too much to care.

With amazement I realized after several weeks in the gym that I could count among my friends some of the most influential men in Indianapolis. Shy Bill Ashpaugh didn't have any trouble talking and joking with some very awesome people. He liked them and they liked him. We were just the good ol' boys of the Olympic Health Club. The only obvious gap was in our ages. I was younger than most of my new buddies and, while they were content to lift weights to keep in shape, they urged me to consider competition. Not that it took much arm-twisting! The old competitive spirit of Westfield's roadside wrestler might have been dormant but it wasn't dead. A gentle prod was all I needed to admit that maybe I *was* ready for a new challenge. Count me in, sign me up, and then stand back!

The neighborhood garage-gym was still in operation and was frequented by a handful of diehard iron pumpers like myself. We decided to form a team, adopt a name—the Noblesville Barbell Club sounded good—and take on the world. Or at least the Midwest.

Because we were of various weights and sizes, we could compete in a variety of classes. We were a complete unit, with a few noticeable shortcomings. Like my body. Although I was determined to win each event I entered, I had watched enough contests to know that I didn't have what is considered the classic weight lifter's physique. I'm far too tall and have small hips. Most successful lifters are short and stocky. If I kept my body weight down to 198 pounds I found myself competing against 5-foot-6-inch powerhouses who had the advantage of concentrated strength. They even *looked* stronger because their muscles bulged from a small frame, emphasizing the contrast. They appeared almost as wide as they were tall. My muscles were spread out over several more inches, giving me a lanky look.

If my weight crept beyond the 198 mark, I was classified as a super heavyweight and must vie with lifters weighing in at 250 and 300 pounds. This problem eventually was recognized by the Amateur Athletic Union and one or two weight classes were added, like stairsteps, to bridge the gap and equalize the competition. But all this would come after I performed my last lift, press, snatch, clean and jerk under the scrutiny of the judges and referee. In the meantime, I existed on salad, fresh fruits, and vegetables to keep my weight carefully in check and within the existing rules. My peanut brittle days were gone for good!

The Noblesville Barbell Club made its first assault on

the world of Olympic weight lifting competition in
Louisville, Kentucky. I'd like to be able to say the city,
amateur athletics in general, and weight lifting in particular have never been the same since. Actually, it was
an inauspicious affair totally unremarked in the pages of
Sports Illustrated. For that matter, even the local news-
papers ignored it. Maybe their reporters got lost on the
way to the gym. We did.

We were all nervous but too intent on preserving our
masculinity to admit it. Full of false bravado, we attempted to cover up our insecurities by exchanging loud
jokes and pretending we couldn't care less about the
contest at hand or the hardware at stake. As we
crossed the bridge over the Ohio River into Kentucky,
the air was pregnant with tension. The voices were
shrill and the laughter seemed forced.

I rested my head against the car window and closed
my eyes in an effort to appear cool and unconcerned
enough that I could actually doze off in the face of the
excitement. Behind the clenched eyelids I amused myself with one of my favorite pastimes—the old "what if"
game. *What if I clutch under pressure and can't lift that
first weight? What if all the other guys on the team go
home with a trophy except me? What if I lose my
concentration and am disqualified for some minor infrac-
tion of the rules? What if the older, more experienced
lifters laugh at me? What if . . .*

I don't know what horrors I expected to greet me
when I walked into the Louisville gym, but the scenario
was totally familiar and comfortable. Lifters in warm-up
suits were going through their pre-contest paces—
bending, stretching, rotating their upper torsos from the
waist, and conditioning their legs by squatting on their
haunches and extending first one leg, then the other.

I staked a claim to a piece of the gym floor and slowly
began to pump up and wind down. Repeating the same

exercises I had done countless times in Indianapolis, Westfield, and Noblesville was reassuring. The faces around me might be new and the backdrop of the old YMCA gym might be different, but the competition rules were the same, the weights were uniform, and the required lifts were standard. No matter what the location, the Olympic barbell would always measure 7-feet-2½-inches long overall and 51½ inches between the inside collars. The handle would always be exactly 1 1/10 inches in diameter.

The criteria for winning were constant whether I was in Louisville or on more familiar turf. I would be allowed three tries at the two lifts—first the snatch and then the clean and jerk. Between the initial two attempts, I could choose how much of a weight increase, ten pounds or more, I wanted. I could also specify the weight increase on the third attempt, as long as it was at least five pounds. If I opted for only a five-pound increase after a successful first try, I would forfeit the third attempt. If I should fail at a lift, I couldn't go back to a lighter weight, but I could have up to three tries at the same weight.

I sized up the competition and decided that maybe, just maybe, I wasn't entirely out of my league, after all. Oh, there were several guys who were heavier and more muscular than I, but there were also a few who probably had endured a lot of sand being kicked in their faces. Beginners. Weekend lifters. Casual competitors.

The difference between the serious and the not-so-serious—the winners and the losers—seemed to be a wonderful air of confidence the contenders shared. They were intense, but not jittery; sure of themselves, but not cocky; spectators, as well as participants. They were totally in control, could study their challengers, "psych" themselves up, and then surpass the field. I watched from the sidelines—a familiar vantage point for me—and I learned. At the end of the day I felt as though

I had attended a crash course in mental discipline. To be a winner you have to think like a winner, feel like a winner, and act like a winner. There was no room for self-doubt or negative attitudes. Sure, strength was important, but it was only one of the necessary components of victory. Determination and confidence were equally important.

When I left Louisville that night, I carried with me not only a beautiful fourth-place trophy—not bad for the first time out—but a valuable lesson in psychology. I was good. And locked in the trunk of the car, I had the shiny, silver trappings of success to prove it.

Three lifters had been better than I in Louisville on that long, long afternoon in September. They were stronger and better disciplined and had gone home with the evidence. But next time would be different. Next time I'd be better. Next time I'd be Number One. If brute strength were what counted, I knew I had the gift. If confidence were the victor's edge, mine grew with each heave of the barbell. If determination were the deciding factor, the kid from Indiana was coming on fast . . .

Chapter 4

DRUGS:
SHORTCUT TO FAME

The headlights of my car caught the tiny green sign marking the Carey Road turnoff. I cut a sharp left, turned off the engine, and coasted into the driveway. It was late and I didn't want to disturb anyone. I could tell by the single lamp left burning in the living room that my parents were asleep, and probably had been for hours.

For as long as I could remember, mom had always left that one light on for us kids as we trickled in late from work or dates. It was like a small beacon in the otherwise darkened, rural countryside. The last one home snapped it off. Tonight I would do the honors. Since Lois and Paul had married and moved to Noblesville, the role of keeper-of-the-light was mine exclusively. I was the lone Ashpaugh offspring left at home.

My brothers and sisters hadn't traveled far from the nest though, with Sam, Shirley, and company just nine miles north at Sheridan, Kay opting for life by the lake at Cicero, and Lois and Dave just over the hill at Noblesville. They might be out of range of the antique bell dad used to ring when he wanted us home for dinner, but a single phone call could set into motion the family telephone chain and a "summit" could convene within fifteen minutes.

I knew the chain would be activated early the next morning when mom, wrapped in her old pink chenille bathrobe, walked into the living room and saw the latest bit of hardware added to my growing collection. It was a beauty—an oversized gold-colored loving cup on a heavy mahogany base. Most important of all was the inscription: *Indiana State Weight Lifting Championship—Second Place, Bill Ashpaugh.*

Mom and dad rarely attended my contests, and when they did, mom spent most of the time wincing, covering her face with her hands, and hiding behind dad. She was convinced I would hurt myself—if not that day, well then, probably the next. Still, they were my most enthusiastic fans—from a distance.

When it came to promoting her son, mom knew no equal. She never complained when the trophies and plaques spilled over from my bedroom, invaded the downstairs, and claimed all available tabletops and china cabinets. She dusted them off, grouping and regrouping them periodically. The most current accolade was always given the place of honor aboard the console radio. It was changed frequently.

After that first contest in Louisville, weekend forays into the world of AAU-sanctioned Olympic weight lifting competition were as regular as our Sunday afternoon family get-togethers and Wednesday evening church services. Every contest brought new titles and new trophies.

Such tangible rewards were symbols of ability, determination, and sheer grit. Adding another statue to the already overpopulated bookshelf or coffee table wasn't important. What really mattered was that every honor meant I had lifted myself—literally—to a new plateau in my sport. I was climbing higher and higher, surpassing the good, better, and best athletes. I was growing stronger, refining my skills, and improving my performance. Every contest was a challenge—not because my mother needed another trophy to dust or to tout to the family and neighbors, but because I needed to know I was moving ... upwards. The competitive spirit I harbored since birth finally had an outlet.

As an athlete I was always in the process of becoming. There was no final destination, just new obstacles. As soon as I progressed to one level, I set my eyes on the next and never rested until I achieved it. When I was named best lifter in Indianapolis, I was happy—even satisfied—for a few days. Then I began looking forward to the next step, the state weight lifting competition. Placing second in that contest was an honor. The field was tough, and I was better than *most* of the lifters. All except one.

As I moved the Indianapolis trophy off the radio and replaced it with the gold loving cup, I reviewed the contest in my mind, lift by lift. What should I have done differently? Where did I go wrong? How could I change my performance next time to come out on top? Before I even shared my second-place victory with my family, I was plotting the following week's match. I snapped off the light only after pledging to try harder, train longer, and improve faster.

I needed a more flexible schedule. Dave and I had discussed many times the advantages of being in business for ourselves—more money, more responsibility, and, most importantly, more flexibility. When you're taking orders from someone else, I decided, it's pretty hard to say, "Excuse me, but I think I'll take the rest of the day off and go to the gym." Instead, whether you're busy or not, you tough it out until 5 P.M., then spend most of every evening trying to catch up with the other guys who have a more leisurely workout schedule.

Still, the idea was frightening. It meant borrowing money we didn't have, with the hope of attracting customers we weren't sure existed. Dave hesitated. And me? Armed with my newly-acquired electrician's license, bolstered by an extra shot of confidence provided by my success in lifting, and spurred by the vision of being my own boss, I usurped the family garage and hung out a shingle that proudly proclaimed "Ashpaugh Electric." A month later Dave acquiesced. Ashpaugh and Ashpaugh. What a duo!

Being an entrepreneur has its advantages. If I stretched my lunch hour into a snack-plus-training break, I merely worked later in the evening to make up for lost time. No clock to punch. No problems to solve. Well, hardly any. But its drawbacks, as we quickly learned, included such things as accounts payable, accounts receivable, purchase orders, filing, scheduling jobs. Hire a bookkeeper. Whoops, the secretary quit; so, hire another. Hmm, whatever happened to all that free time we expected? However, the balancing act between business and pleasure had its positive side effects. The Noblesville Barbell Club could now extend its sphere of competition beyond a hundred-mile radius. Since I was able to break away earlier on Friday, we began traveling to farther destinations to compete. Our central location allowed us to drive to Ohio, Illinois, and Kentucky in a weekend. The end result was added experience and yes, added trophies. Clear off another tabletop, mom!

More changes. The gym I had come to know as my second home closed its doors and most of its patrons (including me) moved lock, stock, and medicine ball over to Hofmeister's. Physically, it qualified as one step below a hole in the wall, but to persons in the sport, it was the only place to train. Dick the Bruiser thought so, along with every bodybuilding and weight lifting champion to come out of Indianapolis in the 1960s. Not only did it boast expertly handcrafted equipment, but it offered what no other gym in the city possessed—Fred

Hofmeister himself—one of the finest trainers in the country. Under his guidance I began training at least every day and sometimes twice a day.

I found myself living in two worlds. One was centered in Westfield and involved home, my electrical business, family, and church. The second, based in Indianapolis, was peopled by athletes and trainers and involved traveling, working out, and competing. The two worlds seldom merged, and I preferred to keep it that way.

Sometimes I felt as if I were two different people, moving about in my separate worlds. There was Bill Ashpaugh, businessman, and Bill Ashpaugh, weight lifter. Never the twain shall meet. And that was a big mistake.

As I sat wedged in our family pew each Sunday morning, flanked by mom and dad, I seldom stopped to think that what I heard in the sermon might apply to my activities on Monday, Tuesday, Wednesday, Thursday, Friday, and Saturday. My worlds were separate but equal.

It didn't occur to me that the faith taught me as a child and rekindled every Sunday could be an asset as I explored new facets of life far removed from our farm and small rural church. I didn't realize that the lessons I had learned during our bedtime Bible sessions could be the thread that extended into adulthood to hold my life together. In my carefully regimented schedule, religion occupied a small slot on Sunday morning and another on Wednesday evening. Count on me to be there, but don't expect me to carry what I learned back to the gym or on to the next competition.

How does that old saying go? "There's a time and a place for everything." Yes, in addition to my other new skills, I was learning to speak fluent cliché. In some ways I *was* a cliché. A little hollow. A little too slick. Going through the motions long after the meaning of what I was trying to prove had been lost.

On the surface, I never strayed far from being the same person I always had been. I still didn't smoke, drink, or resort to bad language. If I were tempted by the lifestyle of my new friends in the gym or on the contest circuit, I refrained from joining them out of habit, not dedication. The rigid standards, instilled in me by my parents, were being challenged and were loosening up. I no longer was completely at home in my sheltered Westfield world, but neither was I entirely comfortable in the more sophisticated world of competitive sports.

Just like any group of people who share a common passion, weight lifters make up a subculture with its own language, interests, and way of life. Introduce two lifters from entirely different backgrounds and then stand back and watch what happens. You'll be lucky to slip a word in edgewise. Weights are the common denominator and will form a solid basis for a lasting friendship.

As the Noblesville Barbell Club began competing farther and farther beyond its home base, the members began making new acquaintances. The same faces and muscles that were present in Cincinnati one weekend might turn up in Chicago or Evansville the next. Between matches or during warmup sessions, conversations were initiated, tips traded, and advice offered.

One suggestion continued to surface no matter what our locale: "Have you tried taking the pill yet? You won't believe the difference it makes. Everyone's using it." And they were. I noticed the same lifters I had competed against on several occasions suddenly were bigger and stronger. Their muscles were more defined and their stamina seemed greater. The reason? "The pill," they said. Always the pill. It was the winner's edge, and it was available to all of us. All we had to do was ask.

But I didn't have to ask. One afternoon as I was scooping up my sweatclothes and stuffing them into my duffel bag after a workout, one of the trainers approached me.

"Here, take these home and try them," he said, handing me a packet of blue, scored tablets. "They're samples one of the doctors gave me to pass around. See if they help."

When he told me the doctor's name, any doubts I might have had vanished. He was a man I knew well from months of training side by side with him. He was intelligent and had a large practice and a flawless reputation. With an endorsement like that, what did I have to lose?

There were no whispers, no warnings to keep the transaction quiet, no money requested. I thanked the trainer, stuffed the pills down into the duffel, and headed for the parking lot. Still, I felt a tug of guilt, or maybe apprehension, at the idea of taking something artificial to enhance my athletic ability.

The pills stayed in my dresser drawer for several days. While my family didn't frown on taking medication when necessary, we all preferred the natural approach. Mom and dad were of the opinion that if a person ate plenty of homegrown food, got eight hours of sleep at night, and breathed his share of fresh, country air, he would never have much need for pills, tablets, capsules, or tonics. And they had three strapping sons and three healthy daughters to prove their point.

For the first time, my two worlds seemed to clash head-on. I didn't discuss the pill dilemma with my parents because I knew how they would react. My friends in the gym and at the contests took the opposite view. No guilt. No regrets. No fears. I had to admit, they certainly didn't *seem* to suffer any ill effects. In fact, they had never looked better. At least, on the outside.

Finally succumbing to the temptation and the curiosity, I swallowed one of the little blue pills, washed it down with a tumblerful of orange juice, and waited for something either wonderful or terrible to take place. Nothing happened. In a way I was relieved, and in another way, disappointed. The following day, the procedure was easier. Still nothing. Unknown to anyone in the family, I began to take the pills daily.

After about two weeks, I noticed the change. Veins, hardly evident before, began to surface down my arms and legs and across my back. My skin felt hard to the touch. Like a balloon suddenly inflated or a water bottle filled to capacity, the surface of my body became smoother, tighter. I was "pumped up" even before I went through my standard warm-up exercises. And I felt wonderful—bigger, stronger, and more powerful than ever.

I no longer thought of drugs as an illegal shortcut to victory, even though the AAU strictly forbade their use. I didn't feel I was "cheating" by swallowing a pill every morning. After all, was it so different from the vitamins most athletes take by the handful? This was just one more in the long list of helpful training aids to assist the competitor in reaching and maintaining his best form.

It wasn't as if I had forsaken the blood, sweat, and tears part of my regimen. I still spent four or five hours in the gym every day. And I still ate mom's homegrown produce, got eight hours of sleep, and sniffed my fair share of country air. Why, then, did I find it impossible to tell my family I was taking the pills?

The tablets had been a small sample packet and were soon depleted. I decided to visit a doctor in Noblesville to get a prescription in my own name and hopefully to learn more about this "miracle" medication. Imagine

my surprise when I started asking him questions and he
resorted to an oversized book called the *Physician's
Desk Reference* for the answers.

The drug was fairly new, he explained, and the medical community wasn't completely familiar with it. He
pushed the book across the desk so I could read it for
myself. Between the mysterious multisyllabic medical
jargon, I picked out enough words to piece together the
meaning. The pills I was taking were anabolic steroids
and were available in five milligram and two-and-a-
half-milligram dosages. From the description of the tablets, I knew I was taking the higher dosage.

The book went on to explain that steroids are synthet-
ic derivatives of testosterone and their effects are similar to the effects of male sex hormones. The pills would
promote body tissue-building processes and would reverse tissue-depleting processes. They had first been
used successfully during World War II for persons
burned in combat. Steroids helped promote the growth
of new skin. They were also useful in treating arthritis
and were given to pre- and post-surgery patients whose
physical condition needed a boost.

However, the book warned that the accepted adult
dosage was five milligrams daily at first, and then two
and a half milligrams for maintenance. After six weeks
of treatment, there should be an interval of from two to
four weeks before resuming the therapy.

The warning bothered me somewhat. Why was it
necessary to stop taking the pill after six weeks? The
answer had to be that the medicine was strong and
possibly dangerous. If a respite were advised after taking only one pill a day for six weeks, what were the risks
for people taking two, three, and four pills daily for
months? I knew some of my weight lifting friends were
munching them like candy.

Then another sentence caught my eye and put my

mind at ease: "Warning—Anabolic steroids do not enhance athletic ability." That simply was not true. I was
proof positive of the fact that steroids improve an
athlete's prowess. Everyone at the gym had com-
mented on my progress and had noticed the physical
change as well. If this book, this so-called *Physician's
Desk Reference,* provided so little information about
steroids that it could claim they did nothing to enhance
an athlete's ability, then maybe it was wrong on other
counts too. My doctor was right, I concluded. The medical community obviously knew very little about this
"miracle" drug.

More convinced than ever, I asked him to give me an
open-end prescription—one that specified it could be
refilled as needed. He agreed, with the understanding I
would take the recommended dosage for adults, one
pill daily. He also made me promise that I would check
with him if I noticed any adverse side effects. I gladly
complied with both requests, knowing full well that I
knew more than he knew . . . at least when it came to
steroids.

Everywhere I looked I found reinforcement for my
decision to take the pills. A champion powerlifter I knew
told me several members of the Olympic weight lifting
team experimented with anabolic steroids as part of
their training routine. He admitted he used them himself
before retiring from competition and would use them
again if he decided to reenter the sport.

The pills' positive effects were not limited to weight
lifters either. Any athlete who wanted to develop
strength, endurance, and muscularity could benefit
from the drug. The secret, of course, was to overdose.
If I were to follow my doctor's advice and limit my
intake to one pill a day, the effects would be minimal. If
five milligrams daily could bring about minor changes,
just think what ten, fifteen, or twenty milligrams could

do! The possibilities were unlimited for the athlete.

It was easy to know when an increase in dosage was in order. As long as I was winning first-place trophies while taking three pills a day, that was the correct dosage for me. But if I started to slip behind the competition, bringing home second- and third-place honors, it was time to increase the medication. And it was so easy. With my refill-as-needed prescription, I merely walked into the neighborhood pharmacy and handed the druggist the clear plastic vial. "Fill 'er up," I said. And he did. Time after time.

Some of my colleagues at the gym and on the contest circuit wouldn't talk about their "habits." A few of them were ashamed that they relied on artificial means to improve their ability. They preferred to let opponents and spectators believe they were special, that their brawn and talent were natural gifts which they developed through long hours and hard work. Others were silent because they felt guilty. They knew drugs were wrong, even illegal, but they knew they couldn't win without them. And the urge to win was stronger than the guilt and the shame.

It was the desire to be Number One that led most lifters I knew into the drug scene. And it was the need to remain on top that encouraged the athletes to take more and more of the pills.

Several were beginning to experiment with a long-acting anabolic agent which is dissolved in sesame oil for intramuscular injection. Used under a physician's careful scrutiny, the drug is a blessing for patients with certain serious health conditions. But for athletes trying to beat out the field at a weight lifting contest, the injection is pure danger. I was sure I would never be tempted to go to such extremes.

Thanks to a rigid training schedule, dedication to winning, and an added boost provided by some little blue pills, the reputation of the Noblesville Barbell Club was spreading throughout Indiana. When we weren't working out in Indianapolis, we were visiting other gyms around the state to train with lifters we met at contests. We were as much at home in Anderson, Muncie, and New Castle as in our home stomping-ground of Noblesville.

As we became more and more a part of the competitive athletic community, members of the club began branching out into powerlifting—the slow, arduous sport of the squat, bench press, and dead lift. It was different, a new type of challenge, and after years of Olympic lifting, the guys were ready for a change. So was I, for that matter. But powerlifting didn't interest me as much as it did the others. I preferred the explosiveness and faster movement of Olympic lifting, and I was satisfied to stay with it indefinitely. Meanwhile, the team was beginning to splinter off in various directions.

Suddenly I realized I probably had had enough contests. I knew I certainly had enough trophies to last a lifetime. Maybe it was time to retire from active competition. The more I played around with the idea, the more it appealed to me. I would never give up training and keeping in shape, of course, but other pastimes deserved attention, too. Like work, for instance.

Ashpaugh Electric was booming and would probably flourish even more with extra effort from its senior partner. I was ready for a more leisurely pace, uncomplicated by training table diets, early morning workouts, long weekend trips to faraway gyms, and pills. Amid promises to stay in touch, Bill Ashpaugh and the Noblesville Barbell Club parted company. The freedom felt good.

I went back to Hofmeister's gym in a more relaxed frame of mind. The pressure was off and I was ready to lend my expertise to newcomers to the sport who were thinking of entering competition. A lot of "oldtimers" had spent a good many hours with me over the years and now I was ready to repay the debt.

Two or three afternoons a week I'd knock off work early, drive down to Indianapolis, and work out until dinner. Approving of my new routine, Fred Hofmeister suggested I use the time in the gym to concentrate on improving a couple of my weak points, for appearances only. He took stock of my physique, decided I should build up my shoulders and back, and designed a program of exercises to do just that. Such specialization is typical of bodybuilding training.

Before long I found myself working out side by side with a man about my age who was preparing for his first physique contest. Anyone who has ever spent any time in a gym knows the benefits of having a training partner. One person can push the other on to new heights while attaining higher plateaus for himself.

Call it the old competitive spirit, but I began to get caught up in the program. The two trips a week to the gym expanded to three, then four, then five. When someone suggested that I, too, enter the bodybuilding contest, I flatly refused, reminding him that I was retired. Retired? I was working harder than ever. Other bodybuilders who trained at Hofmeister's started to wander over to my corner of the gym and offer me tips. They were preparing for the contest, too, and while a spirit of camaraderie prevailed, there was also an undercurrent of competition. I thrived on it.

Even though I was not interested in becoming Mr. Whatever, I couldn't turn my back on the challenge of surpassing the other guys. I had my share of trophies, but I could never get enough competition. No, I wasn't a bodybuilder and I never would be, I insisted. But I was a winner. Through it all, Fred Hofmeister stood on the sidelines, watching and smiling. He knew me better than anyone. By the time the long-awaited contest came around, I was the undisputed champ. No titles. No loving cups. But I knew, and so did everyone else.

I also knew that I had been wrong, dead wrong, about the sport of bodybuilding. Where had I gotten the idea that this was the pastime of softies? Every muscle in my body yelped in disagreement!

I had learned that not only must a bodybuilder *be* strong, he has to *look* strong as well. His coach must study him like an artist views a mound of clay. Together, the coach and athlete mold the body into the most perfect form possible. This is achieved through special-ized exercises that are designed to build or reduce one part of the body at a time. A person who has thin legs, but a large, muscular back must concentrate on building the legs and merely maintaining the back.

In a contest situation the winner is the man (or woman) with the fewest number of weak points. As in a beauty pageant, it's how the participant comes across on stage that determines who takes the title home. The winner has to make his moves just right, accentuating his strong points, hiding his bad. Dieting is important—the bodybuilder can't eat anything that will hurt the tone of his skin. Then, of course, there's the sun. To emerge victorious, the contestant must be exposed to just the right amount of sun to turn him a perfect bronze.

The day before the contest everyone trudged in for a final workout. I could feel the excitement even though I couldn't share in it. I might be the best, I thought, but it really didn't count. I was like the star football player who had graduated and now must watch the game from the sidelines. All the guys slapped me on the back and told me how lucky I was to be retired and free from all the agony of competition. I laughed and agreed with them.

But if I were so lucky, why did I feel so left out?

Chapter 5

TAKING CHARLIE HOME

I don't remember when Charlie walked into my life. He was such a scrawny little kid, hardly the type who stands out in a crowd, much less a gym. He simply appeared in our backyard one day . . . balancing on those funny bird-legs of his and sort of looking up to me, the hulking weight lifter with all the hardware to prove my worth. He was a senior at Noblesville High School and lived two or three miles over the hill, around the curve and down the street.

"You remember me, don't you?" he asked.

Sorry, Charlie. His face might have been one of the multitudes at Hillside Beach last summer, or part of the backdrop at the drugstore fountain, or perhaps in the panorama of hangers-on at the corner gas station. But, no, I wouldn't rank it up there with Mona Lisa or Steve Reeves.

Along with most of the other kids in the neighborhood, Charlie fancied himself a weight lifter. He had heard via the grapevine that I had a small gym set up in our two-car garage out back, and he wondered if it would be all right for him to stop by every so often to work out. This was an old refrain—one I had heard for years. Most of the boys in Westfield and Noblesville had wandered through my gym at one time or other. Charlie was the latest in the never-ending parade.

Weight lifting was a fad for most teenagers, a passing passion that generally lasted a few months at best. My role in life seemed to be mentor: I could offer a few pointers, play Big Brother, save the parents the price of a Sears thirty-dollar portable gym, and wait until the magic of this phase faded.

"Okay, Charlie, you're on," I said.

I learned almost immediately that he was different. A real diehard. I recognized in him a certain stubborn streak that wouldn't let him quit. I had had it too. Still did, in fact. Night after night, when I came home from the office he'd be in the garage working out. We'd lift side by side long after dark, then I'd hang it up for the evening, leaving Charlie behind to continue solo until the rest of Westfield had gone to bed.

I liked him. In spite of our age difference, we had a lot in common. During our endless training sessions in my makeshift gym, we had deep discussions. And, between panting heaves and red-faced lifts, we solved all the problems of the world. At least our small world. I'd talk about work; Charlie would talk about school; we both talked about the current girls in our lives. The topic of weight lifting was our common link, but it was only a starting point for our friendship. As we shared thoughts, we found we also shared ideals, goals, and aspirations. I was a few steps ahead of him in life and he admired me for what I had been able to achieve in our mutual sport.

Charlie set quite an example for me as well. He had a terrific amount of determination, and nothing, not even the skinniest pair of legs in Indiana, was going to stop him from becoming a champ. I teased him constantly, called him "Bird-legs," and suggested he take up piano or some other sedentary pastime. He laughed and came back with a few choice cracks about my sunken chest and sloping shoulders. But he never gave up.

When he graduated from high school he signed on for

a four-year hitch with the Air Force. I sold my gym equipment and headed for Hofmeister's, quite sure I'd never see Charlie or his bird-legs again.

I should have known better. He kept in touch and stopped by the house whenever he was home on leave. If I wasn't around, he visited with mom. She was a pushover for his charm and welcomed him just like one of the family. The two of them—a real odd couple—would sit around the kitchen table for hours, drinking tea, talking, and doing needlework. For some crazy reason, Charlie liked to relax by doing intricate work with his hands. My mother, always happy to accommodate, taught him to crochet. Many evenings I'd come home from the office to find Charlie regaling mom with tales of life in the military while the two of them collaborated on a lacy doily.

He was still lifting weights and, since I was becoming more and more interested in bodybuilding, we found our common ground expanded. He told me some of the training tips he had picked up in the Air Force, and I updated him on what I had learned at Hofmeister's gym. I couldn't resist reviving his old "Bird-legs" nickname, but we both knew he had literally outgrown it. Years of exercise had remolded his body into a sleek, muscular frame. He was living, walking proof of what weight lifting training can do for a skinny kid. No one would ever dare kick sand in *his* face.

My own athletic career was in the process of gathering a second wind. Although I was the last person to admit it, my experiences at Hofmeister's convinced me I enjoyed the sport of bodybuilding more than weight lifting, and I was beginning to feel that old competitive spark. Talking with Charlie rejuvenated the yearning to pit myself against a field of challengers and to win. Without much coaxing, I cut short my self-imposed retirement and decided to put my new talents to the test.

But first I had a bit of catching up to do. While body-building is related to Olympic lifting and powerlifting, it's a very different sport with its own set of rules. Suddenly I, the accomplished athlete, was back at square one. Oh well, hadn't I been the one who had always said he loved a good challenge? Fortunately, I was surrounded by the best teachers in the business. I started asking questions, listening to the advice of coaches and other athletes, and attending as many physique contests as I could squeeze in on weekends.

I learned it isn't enough to build the perfect body; a winner must also know how to show it to best advantage. The judges—usually seven of them—evaluate each contest entrant on muscularity, symmetry, and presentation. A point system is used and each judge keeps his own score card on individual competitors. *Muscularity,* I was told, is a combination of size, shape, definition, and hardness of the muscles. The body should have a tight-skinned, no-fat appearance with muscle contours emphasized by vascularity. *Symmetry* is the balance and proportion among body parts—the degree of harmony in the physique. Here's where heredity enters into the picture. Some guys are born with large waists, thin shoulders, or undersized legs. The challenge of bodybuilding is to work on the weak points until they are up to the level of the body's assets. *Presentation* involves everything about the competitor that isn't directly related to his physique. It includes grooming, posture, walk, and display. Perhaps most im-portantly, it covers the choice, sequence, and execution of poses.

Did someone say posing? This is the part of body-building that was going to be most difficult for me. From all those years of weight lifting, my physique was fairly good. Oh, I needed to build up my back and shoulders, but the muscles were there and the power and stamina had been developed. But I had had no experience whatsoever in "selling" my appearance onstage in a bathing suit under a posing light.

Again, I turned to the guys in the gym for help. They suggested that I first get a full-length mirror and start practicing some simple, basic poses. I should then blend several of my best poses into a routine, holding each individual stance about five seconds before moving on to the next. It was important to glide from one pose to another in an effortless sweeping motion, taking care not to grit my teeth or grimace. A smile would be a plus.

In a contest, time limits are often set on posing routines and may vary from one to three minutes. Required poses are one front, one side, one back, and one twist. After that, the athlete is on his own.

Just two or three months after I officially switched to bodybuilding, I entered my first contest. At stake was the title of Mr. Indianapolis, 1969, and I was nervous, embarrassed, and downright scared about competing. The sport of bodybuilding was coming on strong in Indiana and the gym was filled to capacity for the judging. Because I represented Hofmeister's, I had a healthy cheering block in my corner. One of the spectators in the Ashpaugh pep section was a girl I was dating at the time, and her presence did little to calm my jittery nerves.

The event lasted all day and night, commencing in the morning with the preliminary judging before a panel of seven men. It was an open contest, which meant it wasn't divided into age or height classes. We were each assigned a number and told to file across the stage in a lineup. I felt like I was part of a cattle show. Next, we were called out one at a time to do our posing routines.

The gym was in total darkness except for the spotlight shining directly on the athlete.

The hometown crowd had turned out in force and, when I mounted the platform, a loud rumble of applause erupted from the darkened gym. From my vantage point I could see little more than a soft haze of smoke settled over a shadowy horizon of cheering, bobbing heads. I knew my friends were out there and I relaxed and decided to enjoy the moment.

The early judging took all day and with every hour that passed, I gained new composure. When the five finalists were announced, I was thrilled as my name was called.

The tension built as the judges called us out separately for one last look. They narrowed the field to three and the excitement increased. My nervous energy hardened into sheer determination as I, one of the final trio, went through my posing routine over and over.

The judges were having a difficult time making their choice, so they called all three of us out together to compare us side by side. A judge would call out for us to turn around, and we did. "Throw an arm shot," they would request, and we would comply. "How about a leg shot?" Okay. With stomachs tied in nervous knots, we did as we were directed, smiling all the time.

After an hour at this exhausting pace, the winner was named. Third place went to Bill Ashpaugh. Not bad for a beginner.

I was hooked. The next day the *Indianapolis Star* ran pictures of the contest, including one of me. Everywhere I went that week I was greeted and treated like a celebrity. Guys on the street, girls at the beach, waitresses in restaurants, customers of our electrical business all shook my hand, slapped me on the back, and offered congratulations. Such attention was heady stuff for the former ninety-pound weakling from Westfield. It stroked my ego, built my confidence, and made me hungry for more.

If there were a negative side to all the excitement, it was the knowledge that I would most likely rekindle my dependence on those powerful little blue pills. Yes, steroids were very much a part of the bodybuilding world too. I had picked up on bits and pieces of conversation in the locker room and knew many of the active competitors depended on the drug to give them that extra boost to put them ahead of the field. If you wanted to win—and who didn't?—you took the chance. Oh well, they hadn't hurt me before. What did I have to lose?

Charlie was discharged from the Air Force the next month and came home brandishing an enviable assortment of military honors and a physique that caused every Hoosier bodybuilder to sit up and take notice.

He was anxious to join me on the contest circuit and I welcomed him into the Hofmeister fold. Sure, we were competitors, but first and foremost, we were friends. It was great to have a sidekick to share driving duties to and from the gym and to train with side by side. I had almost forgotten how much fun he was and how much we had in common. We quickly caught up on the lost years and proceeded from there.

He seemed to have everything going for him—a new career, potential to become the best bodybuilder in the state, and even a special girlfriend who was soon to become his wife. If people can be divided into categories of winners and losers, Charlie would head the list of winners. He had more drive and determination than anyone I ever knew. He was going to be Number One, the best, Mr. Everything.

We both knew that, to make it to the top, an athlete has to put the sport above all other priorities. That means hours and hours of training, willpower to stick to a tough diet, and willingness to risk taking the drug necessary to win. Although we didn't talk much about it, our feelings about steroids were the same. We didn't like them; we wished they never had been introduced into competitive athletics. But as long as our opponents were going to take them, so were we. How else could we hope to keep up with the field? And we were winners. Both of us.

I first saw a wrinkle in Charlie's perfect world one day in late spring when we were in the locker room taking off our sweats after a rigorous workout. He was sitting on a bench, fumbling with a shoestring and telling me about his upcoming wedding.

"You're going to be there, aren't you?" he asked.

"You bet," I said, turning around to look at him. Then I saw it, "Hey, Charlie, what happened to your leg?" I asked, pointing to a large lump on his upper thigh. It was blue and swollen and I could tell by the way he touched it that the pain was overwhelming. He laughed.

"I don't know. Guess I must have dropped some weights on it," he said. But something in his eyes gave him away. He was worried.

Bedridden with a miserable case of flu, I missed his wedding the following Saturday. After all my teasing, I really had wanted to see Charlie in tie and tails, serious for a change. I had even had a couple of jokes in mind to play on the newlyweds.

When he didn't show up at the gym during the two weeks following the wedding, I began to wonder if he were giving up bodybuilding in favor of playing house. Oh well, maybe they had extended the honeymoon, I thought, or maybe Charlie was just suffering from domesticity and wanted to stay close to home and his pretty new bride for a while.

Then one day his dad called me and, in a voice shaking with emotion, said Charlie was in Veterans' Hospital with what the doctors thought might be cancer. Cancer? I remembered the swollen blue lump on his leg and felt sick inside.

"He wants to see you," his father said. "Could you stop by the hospital for a visit? The sooner the better."

I told him I would—of course—but I was in no hurry to keep my promise. It wasn't that I didn't care. Charlie was my best friend. But what could I say to him?

I thought about him constantly, remembering the hours we spent together training first in the little back-yard gym and later in Indianapolis. Everything he cared about would be off-limits now. I couldn't talk about weight lifting, the guys at Hofmeister's, or the contest coming up. We had always shared our dreams for the future, yet suddenly Charlie's future looked terribly fragile. Should I tell him I was sorry? Or should I assure him that everything would work out okay? That seemed so superficial. So empty.

I put off the trip to the hospital as long as I could. Another call from his dad was more a plea than a request. Would I come? Could I hurry?

The first thing I noticed when I walked into Charlie's sterile white room was the outline of his body under the sheet. There was a terrible, terrible void. Only one leg stretched down the length of the bed. All my cheerful dialogue left me. What was that joke I had been saving for him? The smile I had pasted on my face when I pushed open his door must have faded to a look of shock. He seemed to understand and held his hand out to me. I reached for it and sat down next to him. No words were necessary, after all. He understood.

In the few weeks since I had seen him, he had lost several pounds and his face had a different look to it. Pale and gaunt, his cheekbones seemed to protrude and his smile appeared too wide for his thin face. The muscles he had spent most of his life building were still there, but his skin tone was slack and his color had an almost yellow cast.

I suddenly realized how delicate life is and how vulnerable we are. The man lying in front of me had been a healthy, vibrant chunk of humanity one month before. Now he was an invalid, his body wasted by an invisible devourer of flesh.

The competitor in me wanted to fight this battle for Charlie. I was a winner, wasn't I? No opponent had ever been too tough for Bill Ashpaugh. But I knew that against cancer I was powerless. Charlie must have understood my feeling of helplessness because he tried to cheer me up with a joke. What irony! There he was, suffering from incurable cancer, with his leg and hip recently amputated, and his major concern was to make his overgrown buddy feel better. But that was Charlie.

"Wouldn't you know, Bill, it had to get me in my worst part? One of my bird-legs," he whispered with a grin. I looked the other way so he wouldn't see the moisture building in my eyes and spilling out over the lids.

"We're gonna whip this thing, Charlie," I said hoarsely. "Then we'll find a new sport. Something different. Who cares about contests anyway? I'm getting pretty tired of them myself. Maybe we should try fishing. My dad knows a guy . . ."

I was babbling. Empty words strung together to fill the silence I couldn't bear. If I talked fast enough and changed the subject often enough, Charlie wouldn't have time to say the word that was on both our minds. Death. My closest friend was dying, and there was nothing I could do to help him. The best I could offer was to try to share the experience with him and shoulder part of the burden. I was ashamed I hadn't come sooner. My procrastination was just another example of selfishness. From now on, Charlie would come first. It was the least I could do.

After that initial visit with him, I made it a habit to stop by the hospital several times a week. Sometimes I'd run into his parents or his new bride and we'd exchange comments on how well Charlie was doing and how good he looked. Why did we find it necessary to lie? We all knew the truth. Even Charlie. When the hospital could do nothing more for him, he was sent home to die. At least he wouldn't have to do it alone. I'd make sure of that.

Our friendship had new depth. We still joked and teased each other, but now we were more gentle, more mature. Again, Charlie was teaching me a lesson. By the way he was dying, he was showing me how to live—with strength, courage, and acceptance.

We'd sit for hours on his living room floor, watching television or talking about bodybuilding. Although he would never be able to participate again, he didn't waste time feeling sorry for himself. He wanted to know how my training program was going and how the guys at the gym were progressing. He talked about attending the next contest as a spectator. It was a contest we had all expected him to enter and to win. Instead, he planned to sit in the bleachers, with one leg of his trousers hanging limply by the other.

He never made it to the contest. Just seven months after I first noticed that ugly lump on his thigh, Charlie died of cancer. His body weight, which reached its fighting level at 230 pounds, was reduced to 150. I know, because, as a pallbearer, I helped carry Charlie home. It was probably the hardest thing I ever did in my life.

My sorrow couldn't be compared to that of Charlie's parents, who had lost their son, or of his bride, who had lost her new husband. But I was suddenly without my best friend. How many years had we known each other? How many hours had we shared?

Charlie had been on the receiving end of all my great dreams and plans. I told him things I could never bring myself to tell anyone else. He never laughed at my aspiration to be Mr. America. I even told him about Peter Lupus and my hope of following his example and eventually moving to the West Coast. Anyone else would have thought the idea was incredible and scolded me for getting a "big head." Not Charlie. He listened, tossed in a bit of advice here and there, and encouraged me to pursue those dreams and fight for them if I must.

I wanted to win now more than ever, partly for my own sake and partly for Charlie. I thought about the little blue pills we had both taken and wondered if they had had anything to do with his death. No, that was too negative, and Charlie was always so positive. He had been a winner right up until the end. I'd be a winner too. For Charlie.

Chapter 6

SOMETHING'S WRONG

I didn't like what was happening to me, but the strongman couldn't find the strength to change his life style. I needed to re-examine my priorities, but I couldn't find the time. I knew I should switch directions, but I was traveling too fast.

What had started as a very positive preoccupation was rapidly becoming a very negative obsession. Weight lifting and bodybuilding are sports—nothing more, nothing less—but to me they had become my entire world. Everything I did was geared toward those four or five hours I spent in the gym each day.

My work schedule was planned around my training program. Ashpaugh Electric Company was successful enough that we now employed a force of twenty. This translated into fewer demands on my time and freed me for more hours at Hofmeister's. Most of my friends were involved in the sport in one way or another. Our conversation revolved around our common interest; the books and magazines we read were related to athletics; our weekends were spent in competition. Although I was traveling more than I ever had, seeing new places, making new friends, my world was becoming smaller and more tightly defined; the boundaries, closer.

Because my family didn't share in this world, I was straying farther and farther from them. Our little white farmhouse on Carey Road was still home base, but it had become merely a place to collapse after an eight-hour day at work and five hours in the gym. Meals were caught on the run and seldom were the old-fashioned, sit-down variety.

Even the great Sunday get-togethers with all the relatives in tow weren't the same. Fried chicken was *verboten* to a training table diet and apple pie à la mode definitely wasn't included in a bodybuilder's regimen. Make mine tuna and carrot sticks, please, with a side order of raw eggs! Some days I managed to swallow two dozen of them, all in the interest of better health, of course.

Often I was the first to stir in the morning and was out the door before anyone else was up. If it weren't for the pot of strong black coffee I left brewing on the stove, mom might never have felt my presence. By the time I'd tiptoe through the house at night, all the lights had been extinguished except the traditional parlor lamp. As I turned it off, I could hear the soft, relaxed breathing of my two sleeping parents in the downstairs bedroom. Only then was I jarred to reality, remembering I hadn't seen them all day.

One night, mom surprised me by waiting up for me. I found her wrapped in her long, pink robe, dozing on the couch.

"Got time for a little talk?" she asked, sleepily.

Hmmm, is it a talk or a lecture that she has in mind, I wondered. I felt guilty about the lack of time I was spending with my family. Sure, I knew I was losing touch, but a guy has to make choices, right? My time to excel as an athlete was *now.* I had years and years ahead of me to be Super Son. After my competitive career was over I could settle down, share more of the burden of Ashpaugh Electric with Dave, help dad around the farm, and even enjoy the expanding crop of nieces and nephews that my sisters and brothers were providing. Maybe I could contribute an Ashpaugh or two of my own. But not now. *Now* belonged to me.

"Remember when we used to sit here at night and read the Bible together and sing?" Mom laughed and motioned for me to sit down next to her. "You were awful. The girls would giggle and wriggle and you boys would pinch and tickle each other. It was the only time I came close to getting you all in the same place at the same time.

"I never told you this, Bill, but you were the one I always thought might decide to go into the ministry. I felt God was going to use you in some way. I guess I got that idea from all those years I taught Sunday School. I found out that the most mischievous kid usually turned out to be the best. That kind of youngster has a strong will and it's hard to break it. It's also hard for Satan to break it. But when a child like that decides to be strong for the Lord, he goes a hundred percent. You could do a lot of good for the church, Bill."

I started to squirm, only this time it was the conversation, not my brothers' antics, that was making me uncomfortable. Why did she put me on the spot like this? Why did I feel so defensive? What she was saying came as no surprise. I had always known she and Dad hoped one of the kids would feel led into the ministry. But not me!

"C'mon, mom, we both know I was never cut out to be a preacher. I like to *live.* I like to be happy. I'd never make it in a black suit, scolding everyone and warning them not to get involved in sports. I'd set a poor example, wouldn't I? Say one thing and do another. I'd be the only pastor around who wore sweats more than a coat and tie. I like to enjoy myself too much. I want to have fun and not feel guilty about it."

The look on her face told me my words had stung.

She didn't lash back at me, though; that wasn't her style. Instead, she huddled quietly, looking down at her worn, red hands. We sat in silence for what seemed to be hours. She, feeling hurt; me, feeling guilty. I almost wished she would yell at me . . . let me have it with both barrels. I deserved it.

"But are you really happy, Bill?" she finally asked softly. "You seem nervous and preoccupied all the time. When you were growing up I could always count on you for a smile or a joke, but now you never sit still long enough for a word. We don't see you. You work night and day, and when you finally come home in the evening, I hear you pacing back and forth upstairs in your bedroom for hours. You'll never know how many times I've wanted to go up and ask you what's wrong."

She was right. I was having a hard time sleeping. I figured it had something to do with the steroids—I was taking seven a day now and they were making me jittery. The doctor had suggested I take two, but that simply wasn't enough to win. So, over the months, I had gradually increased the number. When I had gone back to the doctor and told him I couldn't sleep at night, he had said I should cut down on the pills, maybe taking one a day instead of two. I wonder what he would have done had he known my real daily dosage.

To help me relax, he had given me a prescription for sleeping pills. Before I had realized what was happening, I was taking pills to go to sleep and more pills to wake up. There was nothing illegal about it. Everything was by prescription. But I knew that was a cop-out. I fooled myself into believing that the drug routine was a short-term thing. I needed them now, to get where I wanted to go. As soon as I reached my goal I would kick the habit for good and go back to being the same old Bill again. Only this time, I'd be better. Bodybuilding was like a launching pad that hopefully would catapult me into a larger, better sphere of living. It had worked for Peter Lupus, hadn't it? Why couldn't it work for me too?

"Be patient with me, mom," I whispered. "All my life I've wanted to *be* somebody and now I have the chance. I can't let it pass me by. You'll see. Pretty soon everything will be just like it used to be. Just stick by me a little longer. I've got to get this out of my system."

Childhood dreams—the kind you tuck away and only bring out to savor when you're alone—were starting to bubble to the top. The same thoughts I'd dredged out for entertainment when I had been a child burrowed in the haystack suddenly seemed attainable. Why couldn't I be the strongest man in Indiana? Or in America, for that matter?

I was coming on fast in this sport of mine. Third place in the Mr. Indianapolis contest. Runner-up to Mr. Indiana. I couldn't quit now when everything was starting to come together. All right, it was wrong—dishonest even—to take the pills, but they were a means to an end. Besides, everyone I knew took them. It was the oddball who didn't. Then I'd remember Charlie and the cancer that cut short his race for the top, and my euphoria would wilt like a deflated balloon. But bad breaks always happen to the other guy, I decided. Charlie was just unlucky. Bill wasn't.

Sports had been good to me. The confidence I had so sadly lacked all through school was blossoming. Although I was still shy around people, I forced myself to be more outgoing—first to say hello, to initiate conversation, to greet strangers with a big smile. It couldn't hurt! Through the various personalities I encountered in the gym, I discovered I could talk to almost anyone about almost anything.

Suddenly I realized I *liked* being the center of attention. I enjoyed being listened to, watched for, sought after. When the planners of the Indianapolis 500-mile race asked me to ride a float as a featured guest in the race parade, I didn't hesitate for a moment before saying yes. I was on an ego trip and I was enjoying every mile.

Competitive athletes are a different breed. Most of us have a point to prove. Several, like myself, had been too small in high school to play football and now were out to show the world that they were somebody too. Others might view sports as their only hope of escaping an unbearable situation. A lot of guys who grow up in the ghetto use athletics to launch them into a safer, more comfortable existence. We're all fighters, tough and determined to raise ourselves to the top. Many are self-centered, but we have to be in order to excel.

But I really had no excuse for falling into this glory trap. I didn't come from a broken home or a poverty-stricken background. My roots were firmly established in the wholesome rural heartland of Indiana. My family had always provided a warm, safe cocoon—protective and conducive to growth. But for some reason this wasn't enough. I wanted more. In short, I was a phony, intent upon achieving glory and fame and acquiring all the material trappings possible along the way.

Spiritually, I was only lukewarm. I was worse than the sinner who had never known Jesus. I *knew* Him, had been brought up with Him, had read the Bible from cover to cover. Yet He was only a small part of my life. Oh, I went through the motions of being a Christian. I attended services, gave ten percent of my income to the church, was a Sunday School superintendent, and never went to bed at night without first reading my Bible and getting down on my knees to pray. But I did those things by rote. I had been taught by my parents to do them and they were just as much parts of my daily ritual as brushing my teeth or making that first pot of coffee in the morning, or getting dressed for work.

Sometimes I felt a tug of guilt. I imagined God saying, "But what about your life, Bill?" I'd quiet the Voice by replying, "Not today, Lord. When I get gray-haired, I'll be saved. I'm too busy." So I put God off. My pastor and friends thought I was an admirable man. My mom and dad weren't quite as sure. But God knew I was in trouble.

I'd watch my brothers and sisters stand up at a prayer meeting and sing and testify and I knew they had something I didn't. I was like a faucet that had run dry. Turn me on and nothing came out. I wasn't willing to give a hundred percent. I was uncomfortable with the personal demands of religion. I'd gladly give of my material wealth, but I shirked from giving myself.

I could still remember the revivals I attended as a child when my parents would take me forward to the altar and the preacher would lay his hands on me and say, "This boy is going to work for the Lord."

I backed off. "Not today, Jesus. When I get gray-haired, I'll be saved. I'm too busy." I had too much pride. I wanted to be Mr. Indiana for Bill. I wanted to be Mr. America for Bill.

There were tricks to be learned, some good, some bad, but all geared toward a common goal—winning. At the beginning of every contest I learned to psych out the competition. We all got along well. We were friends. But first and foremost, we were opponents. Every bodybuilder has at least one outstanding physical strong point, and mine was probably my legs. So, while I pumped up before a contest, I made sure my sweatpants were off and I was clad only in my trunks and top. If the judges walked by, fine. In any case, the competition felt threatened and lost a little confidence in their own attributes. Sometimes self-assurance is the edge that puts one participant ahead of the others. My own self-esteem received a tremendous boost the night I was finally named Mr. Indianapolis. Look out, guys, here I come!

I also found out that the smart bodybuilder paces his use of steroids, taking them for about three months before a big contest and getting off them as soon as possible afterwards. Some athletes plan a year in advance which contests they will enter and try to group two or three competitions that are scheduled within a tight time frame. That way, they only have to be on drugs half the year. But at the beginning of a guy's career, he can't afford to be as selective. He has to enter as many meets as possible to build up his reputation. Later, he can ease off and merely maintain his stature within the ranks of the sport. I hadn't reached that pinnacle yet. I was building, stretching my talent, reaching for the top. I had no desire to spend my life in a gym. I wanted to go to Hollywood, get into the movies, follow in the giant footsteps of Steve Reeves, Mickey Hargitay and Peter Lupus. But I was afraid to admit it . . . afraid it would sound too presumptuous.

Finally, a talent agent approached me at Hofmeister's and put into words the dreams I had dreamed for years. Yes, he said, you can make it on the West Coast. Yes, you can be as big or bigger than your heroes. Yes, you can have all the success you ever wanted and more! But there would be compromises, he warned. Important friendships would have to be cultivated along the way. I might have to join the cocktail party set, make myself available to persons who could advance my career, surround myself with glib, smooth-talking, fast-living professionals who inhabit certain undesirable areas of the entertainment world. They wouldn't be the kind of people my mom and dad would understand. But they served a purpose and I would have to play their game until I was in control and could call the shots. Was I willing? Could I put aside the strict moral code of my family? Was it worth it? Just how much was I willing to compromise? How far would I go?

I saw the commitment as a short-term one. I'd never *forget* my conservative upbringing; I'd merely tuck it away for awhile. I could look the other way, turn my back on my parents' high standards until I achieved the success I craved. Then I'd revert to *their* way, the Westfield way. Why couldn't I taste the best of both worlds? Why must everything be reduced to a choice? I wanted it all.

As observant as I was, I failed to see the dark side of this life I wanted. Hypocrisy was the norm, not the exception. Although the use of drugs was strictly prohibited by AAU rules, contest judges knew that nearly all the athletes took them. Yet, nothing was done about it. On the other hand, if an amateur competitor dared to accept five dollars for giving a speech or endorsing a brand of gym shoes, he could be banished from his sport forever.

This double standard was incredible. The athlete who had access to the best supply of drugs went home with the trophy, the judges' blessing, and the crowd's adoration. But don't let the winner make an honest buck on the side to support his involvement in sports or he'll get his knuckles rapped.

Sure, I'm prejudiced in favor of athletes, but I honestly don't believe the drug trap is our own creation. I think it's the public's insistence on seeing the bizarre that has pushed bodybuilders into making freaks of themselves. Fans want to be shocked, excited, and entertained. Such thrills are best provided by extremes: a fiery multi-car pileup on a race track, an explosive rhubarb on the baseball diamond, a no-holds-barred brawl in the wrestling ring. Steady performances can be boring after a while; rules can be inhibiting. The crowd wants thrills—eye-popping, mind-boggling thrills.

Bodybuilders, intoxicated by the applause, titles, and trophies, try to accommodate. Having a healthy, well-developed, natural-looking physique isn't good enough. Too mundane. Fans want the big, bigger, best. Drugs are the answer, even though they can cause nervousness, throw a carefully balanced hormonal system out of kilter, speed up bodily functions to an alarming rate and age one beyond his years. At least for a little while the drug user is king—rewarded by cheers and looks of admiration. The trick is not to worry about what happens next, after the reign is over.

So I decided to make a short-term commitment to this life style with all its injustices and shortcomings. I'd be smart, though, and quit competing when I made it to the top. Then I'd coast, get into show business, and enjoy all the rewards I had coming to me. I'd get my life back in order mentally and spiritually. But right now, I needed a few more titles and a little more exposure.

My immediate concern was the Junior Mr. America contest in New York. This was my first important national competition and I was willing to train day and night in preparation for it. Although my nerves were a little ragged, I was, outwardly, a perfect specimen of health and fitness. Weighing in at 205, my measurements were impressive: biceps, eighteen and a half inches; chest, forty-nine inches; waist, thirty-two inches; thighs, twenty-seven inches, and height six feet. Not bad for a growing boy!

I had been lucky. In all the hours spent in gyms over the years, I had never been seriously injured. Oh, a few bumps and bruises, but nothing to knock me out of competition for long. Minor mishaps are inevitable, however, especially when a guy is training extra hard for a special event. This happened to me while I was preparing for the New York contest. I was tired—exhausted, in fact—from working forty hours a week and putting in two daily training sessions besides.

One night a buddy and I were unwinding after a workout, tossing a medicine ball back and forth before heading for the showers. I got careless and missed my catch, and the gigantic ball careened into my stomach, knocking me flat on the floor mats. Ouch! For a minute or two I writhed in pain while my friend hovered over me with concern. Finally the ache subsided and I was able to follow him into the locker room. Half an hour later the incident was forgotten except for the jokes exchanged between my buddy and me. He claimed I must be in deplorable shape if I couldn't catch a ball from eighteen feet away. I accused him of literally trying to knock me out of the competition so he would have a chance to win for a change!

When I got home that night and flopped into bed for a few hours of sleep, I felt a dull ache in my pelvic area. It was particularly uncomfortable and tender when I rolled over and tried to sleep on my stomach. I remembered the medicine ball incident and smiled. Maybe I *was* out of shape after all. Oh well, I decided, I'll be back to normal in a couple of days.

But a week went by and the pain was still with me. In fact, it was getting more and more persistent. Probably just a pulled muscle or one of those painful under-the-surface bruises, I thought.

Never once did I mention the accident to my family. I knew what their response would be. Mom would shake her head in an I-told-you-so kind of way and my dad would insist I go for a checkup. I didn't have time to worry about myself, much less see a doctor. The contest was getting closer and I wanted to put in my best performance ever. I promised myself if I weren't completely healed by the time I returned from New York, I'd make an appointment and see a doctor. Fair enough? Right on, I decided.

The trip to New York was an eye-opener. This time I wasn't herded from landmark to tourist trap by Westfield High School chaperones, and I didn't have the company of thirty classmates who were equally as naïve as I. No, I was on my own. And what a hick!

It never occurred to me when I arrived at New York's gigantic LaGuardia Airport that I wouldn't be able to return to Indiana that same night after the contest was over. I hadn't made arrangements to get to Islip, site of the competition, and hadn't thought to reserve a motel room for the evening. Luckily, I met a couple of guys at the airport who were going to Islip and had rented a limousine to take them there. Did I want to share expenses? Sure, count me in. Not until we arrived at the gym did I realize what I had gotten myself into. The limo ride had cost more than the airfare between Indy and New York. Hmmm, this country boy had just learned his first lesson! I dug deep into my jeans to come up with my portion.

Lesson number two: Beware of certain types of people who frequent bodybuilding contests. Again, chalk it up to my sheltered Hoosier upbringing, but I honestly didn't know that homosexual men are often attracted to athletes, particularly bodybuilders.

When a photographer who was covering the event for a sports magazine approached me and suggested our having dinner together I accepted, happy to have some company in a strange city. Fortunately, one of the more sophisticated athletes in the contest took me aside and told me that, while Ed was well-known and well-liked on the contest circuit, he was a homosexual who particularly enjoyed befriending newcomers to the scene. He usually suggested dinner and then offered accommodations for the night. I would be especially good prey since I hadn't had the sense to get a room in advance.

What should I do? I didn't want to hurt anyone's feelings or appear foolish and naïve in front of my new peers.

By checking around, I was able to learn where Ed was staying. I phoned the reservation desk and had a room held in my name. After the contest we went out for dinner and then drove back to his motel. When he offered to share his room for the night, I quickly produced a key and said, "Thanks, but I have a room just down the hall." We parted friends and I hurried to my suite and locked the door. Whew! You learn something every day.

I didn't do very well at the Islip contest. My energy level seemed to be very low and I felt tired, even though I continued to get my usual eight hours of sleep every night.

The tenderness I had experienced in my groin area ever since the medicine ball incident finally took shape in a small knot. It hurt constantly. Each time I touched it, I winced in pain. Still, I couldn't stop feeling it, hoping it would disappear by some miracle. It was sort of like having a throbbing toothache and not being able to stop your tongue from brushing over it, though each contact causes agony.

On the flight back to Indianapolis, I couldn't get comfortable in the seat. I'd move first this way and then that, cross my legs, then uncross them. Nothing helped. I could hardly bear to sit still. I remembered my promise to myself to see a doctor if the pain wasn't gone by the time the New York contest was over. The fact that I had placed fifteenth in the field convinced me something was wrong. Okay, okay, I decided. Tomorrow I call a doctor.

I still didn't tell my family. Frankly, I was scared, and I thought my fear would only be compounded by concerned looks from the people I loved most. I was still fiercely independent and preferred to keep to myself. Besides, the upbeat, noisy happiness of all my sisters, brothers, their spouses and children helped me forget the pain and the fear. At least for a little while. If they knew about the lump in my side and the agony I felt every time I moved, they would be too quiet, solicitous, worried. That would be worse than the hurt.

What doctor should I go to? Our family doctor in Noblesville? No, he was too close to home. The doctor who had given me the steroids? No, he would ask how deeply I was involved in the drugs and I would have to tell him. Suddenly I remembered a doctor on the south side of Indianapolis who trained at Hofmeister's.

I had known him for months, although I had never thought of him in a professional sense before. He was just another one of the guys at the gym. Surely, as a friend, he could sandwich me in between appointments so I wouldn't have to wait much longer to find out what was wrong. Eight weeks had passed since the medicine ball hit me, and I was feeling more uncomfortable every day. I called, and he agreed to see me the next day.

"It's nothing, is it, Doc?" I asked in my most offhand manner as I stretched out on the narrow white examination table. "I've been having these terrible nightmares. Guess I've never gotten over what happened to Charlie. As if I'd ever have that problem! You remember Charlie, don't you, Doc? He was my best friend. Like a brother. Some guys seem to get all the bad breaks. Me, I've always been lucky."

Doc looked different. So serious. He checked me carefully, gently touching the knot and pushing down on the area around the swelling. Why didn't he laugh and joke like he did at the gym? Oh well, maybe this was his bedside manner or whatever they call it.

"I want you to see a specialist, Bill," he said, ignoring my silly small talk. "Let me set up an appointment for you right now."

For a split second I felt the strange sensation of having gone through all this before. *Deja vu,* they call it. Somehow, somewhere, I had heard Doc's words before. Had it been in a dream? Or a nightmare? The script was the same, but I couldn't remember the ending. Charlie's face—thin and pale—flashed across my mind. I could see him sitting on the floor talking with me, his empty pants' leg crumpled under his wasted frame.

Get hold of yourself, I thought. *I'm Bill, not Charlie. I'm the lucky one, remember? Sure, I'll see another doctor and he'll probably laugh and tell me I've got a muscle spasm; then he'll give me some medicine and send me home. Maybe I'll have to miss a few workouts, or even a contest or two. I need to slow down anyway,* I told myself. I slapped Jerry on the shoulder and told him I'd see him at Hofmeister's in a day or so. Why didn't he smile?

Dr. Gabrielsen was waiting for me when I arrived at his office the next day. We made casual conversation as he carefully examined me, pausing every now and then to make a note on my chart. He asked a lot of questions, some related to the accident, and some more diverse. Still, I knew with Dr. Ted nothing was wasted. He knew exactly what he was doing and where he was going with every touch and every word.

"What are your plans tonight, Bill?" he asked.

"I'm doing a weight lifting show over at Warren Central High School. Why?"

"What time will it be over?"

"I don't know. Probably around 8:30."

Without explanation, he walked into the next room where he picked up a telephone and told his receptionist to get Methodist Hospital on the line. After a pause, he calmly gave the orders that, unknown to me, would change my entire life.

"This is Dr. Gabrielsen. I want a room ready for Bill Ashpaugh. He'll be there a little after nine tonight."

I felt my world tumbling in around me and I was helpless to do anything about it. I didn't need a degree in medicine to figure out something was terribly wrong. Why else was I told to report to Methodist Hospital in just a few hours? I felt I had lost all control of my destiny. I was traveling on automatic pilot. My choices were gone.

I had to do the weight lifting show—a gymful of kids was waiting across town and they wouldn't understand my being sick. They expected to be entertained and I was obliged to deliver that entertainment. Parents had formed committees, printed tickets, painted posters. It didn't matter that my knees were weak with fear and I could hardly swallow because of the lump in my throat. My life was all planned for me—at least, the next several hours—and all I could do was run through the motions. All according to the script. I would do the show, and then I would report to the hospital, right on schedule. People were waiting for me there too.

I wanted to run . . . turn my back on everything and everyone and jump in my car and drive as far away as I could. But all my problems would go with me: the knot in my side, the lump in my throat, and the terrible fears in my head. I was trapped. All I could do was give up and give in. But to what? Cancer? The very word made me sick with terror. All I could think of was Charlie.

Chapter 7

STRONG MEN DON'T CRY

Like the reels of an old-time film which spin too quickly, my life was moving in double time. That last evening whirled by so fast I wanted to yell for it to stop. I felt I couldn't catch my breath. I wanted to look around, savoring and enjoying everything I had taken for granted up until that minute.

It was so hot that steam from the asphalt settled like a low cloud over the parking lot. Still, I snapped off the air conditioner in my car and rolled down all the windows so I could smell the spring air, warm and heavy with moisture. In the distance, I could see farmers working past dusk, dark shadows hunched on top of bulky pieces of equipment, churning up rich fields and planting long, sweeping rows of soybeans and early corn. All signs pointed to a good season and a record August-September harvest.

I knew my parents, unaware of what was happening to me, were busily setting out the tomato starts mom had nurtured from seeds in cut-off milk cartons that had lined the periphery of our sun-drenched porch for weeks. How often I had promised dad to help out in the garden but had never quite found time! If only I could have another chance!

Suddenly, the simplest task seemed important and worthy of cherishing. I longed to go home and sit down with my parents to one of mom's hearty country meals—sausage, biscuits, thick tangy gravy, homemade applesauce, and great pitcherfuls of fresh milk. I wanted to walk around the farm with dad and stop by Ashpaugh Electric to pass the time with Dave. I wanted to meander down to the corner drugstore and sit at the counter and eat a Tin Roof or slurp a Black Cow and talk about Cincinnati's chances for the pennant this year. I wanted to push my bed close to the open window and fall asleep under the stars.

But now those days were over. I had had my chance and now it was too late. Now I had to do as I was told. Go to the high school; go to the hospital.

The show at the gym ran overtime. I was determined to give it everything I had, and the kids responded with cheers and yells for more. I did a posing routine, lifted a few weights and then dug deep into my bag of tricks and pulled out a few gee-whiz stunts. I bent a steel bar, blew up a hot-water bottle until it burst, and invited a few of the dads on stage to try to force my locked arms apart.

I stuck around after the performance to visit individually with some of the boys and sign autographs. Kids need heroes and if I filled the bill I was happy to oblige. I might not be the idol they thought I was—white knights generally don't take drugs—but at least, physically, I looked the part. They didn't need to know that every movement sent piercing pains through my body; that my nerves forced my hands to clutch each other in an effort to keep from shaking; that my head ached from tension and fear.

I wanted to hold on to the night and to the crowd. As long as the audience lingered, I wouldn't have to excuse myself and go to the hospital. Finally, the last father-son duo said good night and left me alone. No more excuses. No more reasons for procrastination. I had an appointment and time was running out.

On the way to Methodist I stopped at a phone booth and called Dave. I asked him to drive by the farmhouse and tell mom and dad I wouldn't be home that night. They shouldn't bother to leave a light for me.

"Don't get them upset if you can help it," I pleaded. "Tell them something's wrong and the doctor wants to run a couple of tests. Make it sound real routine, okay? I'll call them tomorrow and explain everything."

Dave was stunned—although I had lived with the pain and the lump for eight weeks, this was the first he had heard of my problems. He started asking questions and I had to admit I didn't have the answers. The doctors I had seen were the best, I assured him, but they were worried too. That's why they didn't want to waste any time.

I told him a long needle had been inserted into the painful lump during one examination in an attempt to draw fluid from it. Nothing came out; the knot was a solid mass, and that was a bad sign. "I'll know more tomorrow," I said, "I'll call and tell you then. Right now I gotta go. They're waiting for me at the hospital." I walked to my car and began the lonely drive across town to Methodist Hospital.

Room 232B, on the second floor of the old part of Methodist, was to be my home for the next few days. The fewer the better, I decided, as I stretched out on the narrow, firm bed. It was a private room, overlooking Capitol Street, and probably because of its age, seemed a little more homey than the rest of the gigantic medical complex. It didn't smack quite so much of a sterile big-city institution.

Nervously, I embarked on an immediate mini-tour, opening doors and peeking around corners to get a better feel for the place. One door revealed a small, efficient washroom. The next brought me in contact with a race-car driver being treated for burns sustained in a wreck. He was on the mend and welcomed a new face and a new friend. We hit it off right away. We quickly determined we had something in common. With Indianapolis 500 race festivities in high gear, we were two would-be participants who had had to bow out at the last minute.

No, I wouldn't be riding in the back seat of a convertible and waving to 500 Parade fans after all. Mr. Indianapolis would be watching the marching bands and the floats from his perch atop Methodist Hospital. And my new friend, the race-car driver, would have to miss all the action in the pits and along gasoline alley this year. Instead, he would follow the race on the radio, from his bed.

"Oh well," he reasoned, "look on the bright side. The food's not bad, the service is good, and the backrubs are terrific. All you have to do is whistle, or rather, buzz."

To prove his point, he pressed a button. When a young student nurse presented herself, he suggested a cool, alcohol backrub might be just the medicine for his nervous new friend, Bill Ashpaugh. Yep, this guy and I were going to get along just fine.

I was beginning to unwind, and some of my old confidence came bouncing back. When the surgeon stopped by my room later that night, I heard his explanation of the next morning's surgical procedure and made a half-hearted attempt to joke about it. He told me I would be put under a general anesthesia and a small incision would be made in my left side. The lump, located in my left testicle, would be examined and taken to the pathology lab for a biopsy.

"Try and keep the incision under the trunks, Doc," I inserted. "I'm supposed to compete in the Mr. Indiana contest in a few weeks."

The operation was called an orchidectomy and would

determine if the lump was a cyst or a tumor. If it were a tumor, the lab would be able to tell whether or not the mass was malignant. Also under scrutiny would be the epididymis—the cords resting upon and alongside the testicle. If cancer cells were present, the doctor explained, he had to know their exact extent. He tried to assure me I was in excellent condition to undergo surgery. All vital signs were strong—blood pressure was 150 over 60; pulse was 72, and the standard x-rays which the hospital required of all patients were clear.

"Besides that," he said, "you have a remarkable physique. Strong as an ox, I'll bet."

After he left, I lay for hours mulling over his words. My body—"strong as an ox"—refused to respond to the sedative the nurse cajoled me into swallowing. Long past midnight I stared at the ceiling, my concentration interrupted only by the muted squish of gum-soled shoes as hospital staff members padded down the old terrazzo floors of the halls.

I was like two people in conflict with each other. First, I felt frightened and alone like a child left in a strange place to face an unknown enemy. Then my mood would shift, and the other Bill would emerge— brash, confident, and anxious to get this ordeal over so he might get on with his life. I argued with myself in husky whispers.

"I'm in good shape. The doctor said so himself," said the self-assured Bill. "Besides, I'm young. Who ever heard of a guy my age having some terrible, incurable disease?"

"But there was Charlie," responded the other, more frightened Bill. "Don't forget him."

As if I ever could.

The Ashpaugh family was out in full strength the next morning. Mom and dad came early, bringing a duffel bag full of shaving gear and other necessities I hadn't had time to collect. My sisters weren't far behind, and our pastor and assistant pastor brought up the tail end of the Westfield entourage.

The Bill who greeted the steady stream of visitors from his bed was the self-assured, laugh-a-minute version. When our minister asked if he might say a prayer for me before I entered surgery, I was polite on the surface, but doubtful on the inside. *Who needs prayers?* I thought. *I've got the best surgeons around. I don't need anything else.*

The doctor who had referred me to Dr. Gabrielsen called from his office to wish me luck. Luck? Who needs it? "Hey, man, I'll see you at the gym by the end of the week," I promised.

Two orderlies came to transport me to the operating room, but instead of finding a subdued patient ready for surgery, they were greeted by a stand-up comic who, for this gig, happened to be on his back. We traded quips about my "terrible" legs, and I left them laughing, as a team of masked surgical nurses squired me into OR. But I wasn't done by a long shot.

The pre-op sedative did little more than loosen my tongue. I told the slightly out-of-focus circle of green-gowned professionals that I was a winner. Always had been; always would be. This was just another contest, and I'd come out on top.

A shot of Sodium Pentothal did little more than dull my senses and thicken my speech.

"You can't keep this guy down," I insisted. "I'm going to be Mr. Indiana and then I'm going for Mr. America. Before I'm done I'll be in Hollywood. My agent says I'm star material."

A second dose of Pentothal annihilated my resistance and silenced my bravado. It felt as though a bomb had gone off in my head, and a little nurse held onto both temples to prevent my thrashing around. I settled into a deep sleep, full of dreams of victory and winning. I was in good hands. The best, in fact. Never once did I think to offer a prayer for help, strength, or guidance.

When I woke up several hours later in the recovery room, my head was swimming. I could hardly make out the individual faces of the wall-to-wall people crowded in the room. I was still dizzy, but almost immediately I began talking about myself.

Like a broken record, my refrain was an old, worn-out one. *Bill this* and *Bill that*. I droned on about all the things I wanted in life and how I planned to get them. I drifted back and forth into consciousness while my audience—my family—hovered over me, held my hand, and mopped my perspiring forehead.

The doctor ducked in and called my mom and dad out to the hall. When they returned, mom was crying and dad looked somber. I heard whispers between my sisters but I couldn't concentrate hard enough to decipher the words. "Tomorrow," they kept saying, "the lab tests will be done tomorrow." I lapsed into a deep sleep.

Sometime during the night I must have been moved, because the next time I opened my eyes I was back in 232B with the sun pouring through the window onto my bed. I felt great! The sluggishness brought on by the anesthesia had run its course and I was alert and full of energy. I wanted to go home. The bad dream was over and I was ready to pick up where I had left off. Let's see, what day was it anyway? If I hurried, I might make it home for lunch.

I slipped my hand down under the sheet and gently explored the painful area. The lump was gone! I had won again. I kicked the blanket off and looked. The doctor had done as I requested—the incision was well below the trunks, but the cut was a good eight inches long, right across my lower abdomen. That hadn't been part of the plan. At least, not *my* plan!

A nurse came in, all smiles, and with the usual greeting, " 'Morning, Bill. How ya feeling today?"

"Hey, what's this all about?" I asked, pointing to the long row of sutures. She looked uncomfortable, as if she didn't know what to say, and quickly disappeared from the room. Something was going on and I meant to find out what it was. Then the surgeon came in and sat on the edge of my bed, and said, "Bill, I've got some bad news for you."

"Go ahead, Doc!"

"The tumor's gone, Bill," he began.

"I can see that," I retorted. "But what's this big cut for? I thought you were just doing some routine test or something."

"You don't understand," he said. "The tumor was malignant."

His words seemed cold and cruel, but he was only being honest. For once in my life I couldn't think of anything to say. I hadn't won after all.

"You going to take me back in and cut on me again?"

"I think we're going to have to, Bill."

I thought for a minute of all those hundreds of tiny blue pills I had taken. I remembered my first visit to the doctor when I asked him for a prescription. He had taken down a big book from the shelf and read me the side effects of steroids. He asked me if anyone in my family had ever had cancer.

Why? Was there some link? At the time I hadn't cared. All I had thought about had been winning. Well, now I had lost the big one and nothing else mattered. Bodybuilding. Weight lifting. How silly they seemed! Had I given up my life for a collection of tarnished trophies and a string of faded satin ribbons? The laugh was on me. I was the biggest loser of all because I had been so stupid. I had traded so much for so little.

The doctor left and cornered my family out in the corridor. More whispers. Mom and dad hurried in, full of apologies. They had tried to get to the hospital before the doctor could tell me the bad news. They hadn't wanted me to hear it from him; in fact, they hadn't wanted me to hear it at all. They weren't sure I could handle it. And they were right.

One by one they all clustered around my bed, starting with Lois Anne, not so little anymore, and on up to my parents. Where were the smiles, the jokes, the noisy laughter? They looked serious as each one tried hard to say the right thing.

"How you doin', Bill?"

"Can I get you anything?"

"The phone's been ringing off the hook with people calling to see if you're okay."

The last to speak was mom. Like most mothers, mine comes equipped with a special kind of radar. No matter how hard I try to fool her, she always knows exactly what's going on in my heart and in my mind.

"You're not in very good shape today, are you, Bill?"

"Not today, mom." *Strong men don't cry,* I thought. Even as a kid I had never been able to cry, yet I knew the tears were going to come. I pulled the pillow from behind my head and put it over my face. I squeezed it hard to muffle the sound. I was dying.

All my beautiful dreams would stay dreams. Never realized. I had come a long way; in another year I would have won everything. So close. I had come so close. Now it was over. No one could get me out of this jam. My family, who had always protected me and made life easy for me, was powerless. So was I. This was my battle and I was going to lose it.

One by one they broke down and cried. I heard them slip out of the room and make their way down the wooden halls. Finally alone, I let the tears come un-

checked in great waves. Still I clutched the pillow over
my face so no one passing the door could see or hear
me. Even in the darkest moment of my life, I couldn't
forget my pride. My shoulders shook uncontrollably and
my breath came in great gasps. I cried like I had never
cried in my life.

Then I felt a little tug on the sleeve of my pajama shirt.
No one had come in; I knew that for certain. Whoever it
was had never left. I felt the pillow being lifted away
from my face. Lois. With tears streaming down her
face—her beautiful, grown-up face—she sat close to
the bed. She took my hand and put it against her wet
cheek. She was crying, too, but she had a joyful look.

"Bill, Jesus Christ can heal you."

She looked so pretty, almost radiant. My kid sister
who had always turned to me for the answers was now
offering a solution to the toughest problem I ever faced.
I felt like a man falling through space. Jesus Christ was
there, but he was so small in my life. Still, I reached out
and grabbed and held on for all I was worth. I didn't
know much about Him, but He was all I had left.

"Lois, what are you saying?"

"God can heal you of this cancer just as easily as He
can heal you of a cold."

"You mean like He did in the Bible days?" I asked
doubtfully.

"Just like that."

All my life I had let God down. I used to laugh and
make fun of evangelists who said they could heal sick
people. I couldn't relate to all that hocus-pocus. I had
always wanted to be good, to be spiritually inclined. But
not enough to do anything about it. I wanted to be
helpful to people, I really did. But I was never willing to
go out of my way. Now Lois was telling me Jesus could
heal me. Me? Why should He want to? What had I ever
done to deserve a miracle? I never thought God knew

much about Bill Ashpaugh. Or cared.

"Lois, do you think He can take this cancer out of me?" I whispered.

"I know He can."

I had had a bath right before surgery and was lying between two freshly laundered sheets, yet suddenly I was overcome with a terribly dirty feeling. I felt so small and inferior. I felt as if I were in the presence of God and I wanted desperately to say something to Him. It was as if Lois wasn't in the room anymore. Nothing mattered except Him and what I felt in my heart.

"God, you know I've been a phony all my life. But I feel different now. If You'll accept me today, if You'll come into my life, I'll give You everything I've got."

Looking back, I realize I hadn't offered Him much of a bargain. I was a nervous, unhappy person who had just been told he had cancer. No, He wasn't getting a very good deal at all.

"I want You in my life, God, and I'll do or say anything You want me to. I'll quit lifting weights—anything—if only You'll come into my life."

I never asked Him to heal me. I forgot about the cancer because I was suffering from something much worse and had never realized it until that moment. I lacked peace of mind and heart. My spirit needed God far more than my body did, and at last I knew it.

It happened. I don't know how. But like the blind man in the Bible, suddenly I could see. I looked up at Lois, my beautiful baby sister, and smiled and cried at the same time.

"I've got Jesus in my life."

I gave Him everything that morning, including my pride. Most importantly, I gave Him all of *me*. I knew I was ready for heaven—something I had never been sure of before. And for the first time, I wasn't afraid to go there. Whatever He wanted was what I wanted too.

"God, I know if I die right now, You're waiting for me. I want to go, but if You want me to stay here I'll work for You."

I felt a wonderful, comforting peace wash over me. I wasn't worried or nervous; I didn't have to pace the floor or wring my hands in fear. Total submission. Total freedom. How good it felt. When mom came back she could sense the change in me. I asked her what the doctors told her, and she saw I had the strength to hear. They gave me six months to live without surgery; longer, if I agreed to an operation. They were going to give me a full report tomorrow when all the lab test data had been compiled. Could I take it? Yesterday, no; today, yes.

I got up and put on my street clothes. Sure, I was in pain but I wouldn't give in. The sutures tugged at my stomach as I slowly pulled on a pair of khaki slacks. My head throbbed from the double dose of anesthesia as I pulled a knit shirt down over my shoulders. But the bed that looked so inviting to my aching body repulsed me, a symbol of defeat. And I was a winner. Always had been. I would sit in that chair until night. When the rest of the world went to bed, so would I. Not a minute sooner.

By the time my last visitor had said goodbye, I was on the verge of collapse. But a happier basket case you've never seen! I crawled into bed and had a long visit with Him. He was like a Big Brother with such broad shoulders to bear all my problems. We talked a long, long time.

I woke up happy and muddled . . . muddled because in my sleepy state I couldn't remember why I felt so great. Wasn't this Methodist Hospital? Right. And hadn't I been told I had cancer? Right again. So why the smiles? Then it all came back to me and I felt even better.

I wasn't alone anymore. I had a lifetime Companion

who was a listening post, a confidante, a helpmate, and a friend. I had a hall full of friends and family waiting to crowd into my room to buoy my spirits, pray with me, laugh with me, and help me get through whatever the day would bring.

But best of all, I had Him. Long after the visitors went home and the lights went off, He would be with me. If I woke up at midnight full of the fears that seemed to plague me only during those eerie pre-dawn hours, He was there to put the problems in perspective. He was at my side at that very moment, and from the looks on the two surgeons' faces entering my room that morning, I was going to need all the support I could muster.

"Bill, you're a man and we're going to talk to you like a man," began one of the doctors, sitting down on the corner of the empty bed. He told me to slip off the hospital gown so he could examine the closed wound.

"Yesterday we removed your left testicle, along with the epididymis cord," he explained. I must have looked baffled because he backtracked and tried to scale down the fifty-cent words into easier, layman's terms.

"Yesterday," he began again, "we removed your testicle and the tissue that supports it. We put them in what we call a specimen container and sent it to the hospital lab where a pathologist examined it under a microscope. I've got the full report here on what he found, Bill, and frankly it isn't very encouraging. The lump that was so painful to you was a malignant teratoma. What that means is it was technically three types of tumors in one. A mixed growth. Any malignant tumor is serious enough, of course, but one of the types you had was a choriocarcinoma, a highly malignant variety. It was large—five and a half centimeters in diameter—and I'd guess it had been there several weeks."

I felt very vulnerable, standing without any clothes on,

hearing what sounded like my death sentence. I scooped up the hospital gown and wrapped it around myself.

"The type of malignancy you had," the doctor continued, "is a fast-spreading kind with great propensity to travel by way of the blood stream or the lymph system. To reduce the chances of its spreading to other parts of your body, we recommend major surgery. Without the operation you may have only six months to a year to live. Even with the surgery we can't make any guarantees. I really wish I could be more encouraging, Bill, but I want to be completely honest with you."

"The type of treatment we suggest is a prophylaxis, a protective treatment, against cancer," interjected the second doctor. "When I use the term 'we,' I mean several doctors who have been asked to consult on your case. The consensus is that you should be taken back into surgery and undergo a major retroperitoneal node dissection, which means that we will follow the major arteries from the rib section all the way down to the pelvic area.

"Time is very important, Bill. Just think how quickly that lump appeared. A few weeks ago it wasn't there. Yet when we removed it yesterday, it was full of deadly cells. Those same cells might be traveling to other parts of your body right now. If we didn't think that to be likely, we wouldn't suggest the surgery. We can't make any promises, but if you agree to the operation, you might have four years added to your life."

As if to underscore the seriousness of my condition, the doctor showed me the pathology reports. Although much of the jargon was gibberish to me, I could pick out enough meaning to know he wasn't exaggerating: *neoplasm, hemorrhagic areas, malignant teratoma, embryonal carcinoma, malignant trophoblastic cells.*

I appreciated his honesty. I knew the information on

those sheets of white paper had been gathered by highly trained professionals during elaborate, carefully supervised testing procedures. I admired and respected the knowledge and dedication of the doctors. But I had to do what I knew was right.

I shook my head. "No, Doc, you're not going to have to cut on me again to make me better. There's a Man Upstairs who's going to do it for you."

The surgeon looked aghast, as if by the "Man Upstairs" I had been talking about a patient on the next floor. I had to laugh at his expression.

"Something wonderful happened to me yesterday, Doc. Jesus came into my life. All I did was ask and He was there. I guess He always had been nearby, but I never took time to see. I feel great! I think He's going to heal me. No, I *know* He's going to heal me. It may take time. I might not look too good to you yet, but I'll be all right. I appreciate everything you've done for me—you, the other doctors, the nurses, and the hospital—I really do, but I think we can take it from here."

"Bill, we're talking about your *life,*" he urged. "Don't throw it away."

"I don't intend to, not now that I've finally figured out what it's all about. A week ago my life wasn't worth a nickel, Doc. But today, I'm a whole new person. I plan to hold onto it, believe me."

The doctors exchanged glances. They were somber while I was all smiles. "Is there anything we can say to convince you . . . ?" one of them began.

"No way," I replied.

"Okay, Bill, tell you what we'll do. Stay here just a couple more days to get your strength back. Then go home for a while and think it over. Come back in thirty days and we'll run a lymphangiogram to check on the cancer's spread. Maybe by then you'll reconsider and let us help you. Fair enough?"

"Fair enough."

They left, convinced, I'm sure, that poor Bill Ashpaugh's problems weren't limited to his pelvic region. His brain could use a little help too.

I hardly had time to shave and put on a fresh shirt and jeans—no hospital gown for this guy—before the pastor and assistant pastor of our church walked in. From the pained, grief-stricken looks on their faces I knew they hadn't come to celebrate my new life and share in my new happiness. No, they were there to bury me, or at least to prepare me to meet my Maker. What they didn't know was that I had met Him the day before and we were both doing fine, thanks. Fortunately, my sisters were right at their heels. The family support system had no intention of failing me now.

"Bill, we were so sorry to hear the news," said the pastor in hushed tones. If he fumbled a bit, I couldn't blame him. I wasn't looking the way he had anticipated.

Fully dressed, I was sitting in an easy chair with my legs propped up on the air conditioner. The curtains—shouldn't they be pulled shut to protect the patient from the outside world?—were wide open to let the sun pour in. If the ministers expected to be greeted by a depressing air of death, they were instead bowled over by the scent of Aqua Velva, a gift from one of my nephews, which I splashed on liberally to show my appreciation. The bed—shouldn't the patient be *in* it?—didn't show so much as a wrinkle. Beds were for tired folks or sick people, and I was neither.

"We want to pray for you, Bill," said the pastor.

"Yes, I'd like that," I answered honestly and bowed my head.

"Lord, we don't understand why Bill is being taken from us. But we know he's going to heaven . . ."

I sat there in reverence until the meaning of the prayer sank in. *Hey,* I thought, *this is some sort of farewell speech. I don't want to hear this.*

I glanced over at my sisters for strength. One was rolling her eyes in disbelief, while the others just shook their heads. After the pastors left, mom laid down the law: No more negative visitors, especially from ministers who preached the teachings of the Bible on Sunday mornings and Wednesday evenings but couldn't apply them to everyday life during the rest of the week.

For years I had heard our pastor tell our congregation that God could do anything, that He was the Almighty. Yet, when faced with the human disease of cancer, the minister conceded defeat and merely said goodbye. Were God's miracles just for people who lived hundreds of years ago? I couldn't believe that. Yet, I felt shaken by the ministers' willingness to accept my death.

Mom and dad called a family huddle and decided exactly who should be allowed in my room and who should be gently told that "Bill isn't up to company right now." No more tearful goodbyes from girls I dated, or quivering farewell handshakes from guys at the gym. Only believers would be welcomed from then on. Only positive influences would be invited to come in and bolster my new strength and faith. Books and magazines that stressed the reality of healing in modern times would be gathered from friends and transported to the hospital. Someone would be with me all the time to pray for me, talk with me, and read to me.

The Ashpaughs of Westfield had united forces, devised their battle plan, and were on the attack! What they didn't realize was that their best ally was waiting quietly out in the hall with enough strength and untapped faith for all of us put together.

Chapter 8

NANCY
AND COMPANY

Halting the stream of mourners that filed into Methodist Hospital to pay what they must have considered their final respects to "poor Bill" was no easy task. The visitors meant well, and I loved them for their concern, their cards, their tins of homemade chocolate chip cookies and their great bunches of garden flowers wrapped in cones of wax paper.

There were neighbors from the farm ("I'll never forget the way Bill used to bale hay . . .") , friends from Westfield High School ("Remember me, Bill? I sat behind you in English lit class . . .") and pals from the gym ("You were the best, Bill. Another year and you would have won it all . . ."). Conversation centered on the past, with occasional speculation on what might have been if only, *you* know, hadn't happened. No one could bring himself to say that most hateful and fearsome of all words. *Cancer.*

Instead, condolences were delivered in hushed voices, eyes were downcast, and heads shook from side to side in disbelief. The goodbyes varied in length but were almost invariably punctuated by frequent squeezes of the hand and discreet dabs of the handkerchief. I found myself comforting the comforters. When mom and dad issued the moratorium on visitors, I don't know who was more grateful, the callers or the patient.

Frankly, I think we all deserved a rest.

One visitor who adamantly refused to relinquish her spot outside my room was Nancy, a pretty, dark-haired girl with deep blue eyes, a wide smile, and a stubborn streak that was an even match for the phalanx of Ashpaughs posted at my door to screen would-be mourners. In her quiet unassuming way, Nancy settled in for the duration of my stay, and that was just the way I wanted it. She was special. Very special.

To my family, she was just another girlfriend— younger than some, more attractive than most, but surely no more permanent than the rest. But she was different. I knew it, and they were beginning to find it out. As other girls took their turns saying tearful, overly-dramatic farewells, Nancy kept her emotions carefully under wraps, camouflaged by that terrific smile. As long as she was sitting by my bed, she chattered about people we knew, her job, Al Unser's great victory in the 500-mile race and all the activities we planned to share that summer. Only when she slipped out of my room to the refuge of the busy hospital corridor could I hear her soft, muffled cries. Strength— physical and mental—had always impressed me, and Nancy was a real champ in both divisions.

If you're supposed to meet the love of your life in a romantic setting, against a backdrop of music and glitter, Nancy and I were doomed from our initial encounter. But then, nothing about our courtship was normal since most of it took place in a sterile cubicle in Methodist Hospital. Often as we sat, hand in hand in Room 232B, we laughed about what had to be the most *unromantic* relationship on record. No movie producer would ever badger this couple for the rights to tell its love story on the big screen. In fact, sometimes I'm tempted to embellish the details to make them more glamorous; but no, I'll tell it like it was.

I first spotted Nancy two or three months earlier in a restaurant, with dishes, not bells, clanging in the background. We were hardly dressed for such an auspicious occasion—I was in my Ashpaugh Electric coveralls, my hair still wet from the shower at the gym, and she was jotting down orders for ham sandwiches on rye—hold the mayo—in her waitress' uniform and apron. She immediately let me know she was totally unimpressed with me, my manner, my muscles, and my efforts to sweep her off her tired feet. The lady was all business.

The restaurant wasn't one of my regular watering holes, but it was located across the street from Hofmeister's and offered a quick cup of coffee after practice. A friend and I wandered in one night, keyed-up after a good workout and not quite ready to head home.

"May I help you?" asked the waitress politely. I looked up into one of the prettiest faces I could ever remember seeing. She was poised, with pen and pad in her hand, waiting to take our order.

"Wow," I said, after she hurried off toward the kitchen to pick up a couple of BLTs.

"Bet you can't get a date with her," challenged my buddy, Don. I saw the glint in his eye and grinned.

"Are you saying that I, Bill Ashpaugh, can't get a date with . . . with . . . (I realized I didn't know her name!) that girl?"

"That's right."

"You're on."

Boy, did he win! I summoned all my I'm-just-a-country-boy-from-the-farm charm and, after a couple of *aw-shucks*', offered to drive her home after work.

"Thanks, anyway," she said curtly. "But I have a ride."

Okay, okay, score one round for Don, but I wasn't giving up that easily. Sooner or later Nancy (I'd never forget her name again) would say yes. The challenge was much more than a game; I liked her and wanted to know her better.

For two long weeks I tried to convince her to have dinner with me, see a movie with me, go for a drive with me, *anything!* Even an occasional smile would do, I pleaded. I decided the courting routine was more rigor-ous than lifting weights any day, and the BLTs-at-midnight habit was ruining my training table diet. Three weeks and five pounds later she relented and agreed on her next night off to go out for "half-a-date"—meaning a quick hamburger and then straight home. Oh well, it was a start.

I picked her up that Wednesday afternoon in my old truck. This was a switch for me, who loved the VIP role and all the expensive trappings that went with it. For some reason, I didn't want her to be attracted to me just because I had a fancy sportscar and a wardrobe of over-priced clothes. Nor did I want her to be unduly impressed with my physique. To play the anonymous role to the hilt, I wore my favorite pair of gray Ashpaugh Electric coveralls. It's a wonder her mother let her leave the house with me.

Following Nancy's "half-a-date" rules to the letter, we went to Knobby's, a nearby restaurant, and ordered hamburgers and coffee. I knew I didn't have long to convince her my intentions were honorable and that I wasn't nearly as loud, self-confident, and boorish as my first impression indicated. I decided to be a listener for a change and let *her* do the talking. It was a good choice; I liked what I heard.

Nancy was much younger than I had guessed. She had never really known her dad, and since her mother worked hard to support the family, Nancy wanted to do her share. She was fiercely independent and deter-mined to succeed. We seemed to have more in com-mon than I had hoped.

She wanted to know who Bill Ashpaugh was; where he had been and where he was going. Surprisingly, I didn't have much to say. I found I liked listening to her much better.

If Knobby's revised its free coffee fill-ups policy that night, you can blame the couple in the corner—the girl in pink and the guy in the coveralls. We talked for hours, sipping coffee and learning to be comfortable with each other. I told her about my family, the electrical contracting business that Dave and I started, and about my church. She said she hadn't been raised as a Christian and didn't attend services. She wasn't opposed to religion for other people; it simply didn't have a place in her life.

If she didn't understand my faith, neither did she comprehend my devotion to my sport. Hofmeister's? Bodybuilding? She hadn't heard much about either. I decided to let her think I enjoyed lifting a few weights for fitness and let it go at that. I saw no need to drone on about contests, titles, and trophies. There would be plenty of time for those and other topics later. Suddenly time didn't seem to be such an issue. I was sure Nancy and I would be spending many hours together in the future.

We became a pair, a recognized duo, a real "item." No rings, pins, or promises were exchanged; we simply agreed that we'd rather be together than apart. No words were necessary. Our routine was established: every night after my workout at Hofmeister's I'd walk across the street to the restaurant where Nancy waited tables. I timed it to the minute so I had a chance to grab a cup of coffee while she clocked out, collected her purse and exchanged her uniform for slacks and sweater. Then I'd drive her home where her mother usually had a fresh pot of coffee and a snack waiting for us. More talk would follow; hours and hours of it. We never seemed to tire of trading ideas and sharing feelings.

She was different from any girl I had ever before known. I liked her so much it frightened me. None of my dreams for the Mr. America title and a Hollywood acting career called for a leading lady. I was assured by everyone in the business that a steady girlfriend was a definite liability for someone with my giant aspirations. But it felt so good to unwind and be myself with Nancy.

She liked me for what I was, not what I had. She didn't care which car picked her up for a date, as long as I was at the wheel. She preferred a day at the beach to a night on the town. She was proud of my achievements but not awed by them.

Even when I surprised her by inviting her to the Mr. Indianapolis contest and then turning up on stage as a participant, she kept her sense of humor. She had never been to a bodybuilding show and hadn't seen me in shorts before. Was she impressed? No way.

She may have been my most enthusiastic cheerleader during the competition, but she doled her praise out sparingly after I won the title. No kisses, no idolizing looks, no offers to pose with me for the newspaper photographer. Instead, she whacked me appreciatively on the back and whispered that I sure had funny-looking legs.

I knew I had to make a decision; my relationship with Nancy was crowding my training schedule. Which would it be? If I were to stick to my game plan of entering as many contests as possible to acquire recognition, I needed to devote all my energies to the pursuit of titles. I couldn't be staying up late at night, spending valuable hours escorting a pretty girl around town, seeing too many movies, eating too many hamburgers, and mentally losing sight of my goals and priorities. Too much time had been invested in my dreams to switch directions now.

Somehow I had to free myself from this wonderful habit called Nancy and get back to work.

I didn't want to turn my back on Nancy when she finally was beginning to believe in me and in herself. Rather than face the problem head-on and talk it out, I pretended it didn't exist. I simply decided to stop calling her or seeing her. Without excuses or explanations, I untangled myself from her life. For five long days I removed myself physically from the situation. Then, late one evening I received a call at the gym.

"Bill?" Her voice was soft and controlled, but I could tell she had been crying. "I don't understand what you're doing to me. Was it all an act?"

"Nancy, I'm sorry, I don't want to hurt you . . ."

"If you don't care about me, please, just say so," she whispered, her breath coming in short catches now. "At least be honest with me."

I hung up and ran across the street where I found her crying and looking more like a heartbroken little girl than the sophisticated young woman she tried so hard to be. I told her I was sorry, so sorry, and I would never hurt her again. Although I wasn't sure about anything else in my life, I knew what I said was the truth.

Back together, we began seeing more of each other than before. Again, no promises were made except the one which called for total honesty. I explained to her why I had halted our relationship. She didn't understand my goal of an acting career but she was willing to accept it. She made no demands of me and resigned herself to settling for the "leftover" moments. Time not spent on the job or in the gym belonged to Nancy.

I still felt a minor conflict about our relationship. I wasn't in the market for a wife. Did I say *wife?* No, we had never talked about marriage and I had to get the idea out of my head. Although I spent hours and hours at her house and got along famously with her mother, I refused to return the compliment and invite Nancy to Westfield to visit the Ashpaugh clan. Bringing a girl home to meet mom and dad sounded so serious. So *final!*

Because she was such an understanding listener, Nancy became my favorite sounding board. Long before I mustered the courage to see a doctor about the lump on my side, I told Nancy about it. I couldn't bring myself to tell her exactly where the knot was—I was still too much of a shy country boy to be that specific—but she knew it was causing me physical and mental anguish.

Her advice was sound: I had to seek medical attention. When I procrastinated, she pushed; when I invented all sorts of reasons why I couldn't possibly take the time to see a doctor, she knocked down each excuse with practical logic. Finally, her words and my pain—equally sharp—won out over my stubbornness. I made the doctor's appointment and then stopped by Nancy's restaurant for one last shot of confidence before keeping it.

"I want to go with you," she insisted, doffing her apron and looking around for the owner in anticipation of an early exit.

"No," I said, calming her hands to a slow fidget. "Tell you what I'll do—as soon as the doctor's finished with me I'll come right back and tell you everything that happened. You might as well stay here and keep busy rather than sit in a waiting room imagining the worst."

She agreed, and I hurried off to Dr. Gabrielsen's office. When I returned much later, the rush hour was over and Nancy could sit with me at a quiet back table and hear the bad news.

"He wants me to go into the hospital tonight, right after my show at the high school."

"Good," she replied with relief. I looked at her in surprise. "At least now we'll find out what's wrong. I've been worried sick ever since you told me about the lump,'' she explained. ''Can I go to the hospital with you?''

''No, it'll be so late. If you're not too tired tomorrow morning, why don't you stop by before they start doing tests on me,'' I suggested.

Even though her hours at the restaurant were three 'til midnight, she was at my door at seven the next day.

''Aren't you exhausted?'' I asked. She just smiled that wonderful smile and said she had juggled the schedules around and somehow arranged to take a week of vacation so she could be with me the whole time I was in the hospital.

She wouldn't get in the way, she promised, and she understood that my family had priority as far as visitors go. But couldn't she please just sit down the hall in the waiting room in case I needed her? Would I mind if she ducked in every so often just to see if I wanted anything? In all my misery, I thanked God for Nancy. I must have done something right to have deserved her. Angels surely come in all sizes and shapes and from all walks of life. Mine slipped into my world wrapped in an apron, wearing a big smile, and carrying a BLT.

If I thought Nancy were spunky before, she more than proved her stripes that week. Without causing so much as a ripple in hospital procedure, she managed to break every rule of the house. She arrived daily at 7 A.M.—hours before visitors were allowed in the halls— and stayed until 10 or 11 P.M.—long after the lights-out command.

Since she was just learning to drive and didn't have her license yet, she had to either cajole a friend into doubling as taxi driver or rely on stuffy, wheezing city buses to transport her back and forth between hospital and home.

Often nurses would gently remind her that visiting

hours were over, and Nancy would sheepishly walk toward the elevator, only to return minutes later by way of the stairs. She'd hide behind doors when hospital personnel made the final bed check before turning the lights down, then she'd park herself in the chair next to my bed and talk or read me to sleep.

One morning the grueling routine got to her, and she slept through her alarm clock. When she hadn't arrived at the hospital by nine, I panicked and called her. "Where are you?" I demanded of the owner of the sleepy voice on the phone.

Within half an hour she was at the door looking in at a very sheepish patient. I was upset with myself on two counts: first, for having wakened her; and second, for not being able to cope with her absence. No doubt about it, I was getting very serious about this angel of mine.

Taking my cue from Nancy, I began concocting a few hospital high jinks of my own. Since I insisted on wearing street clothes rather than pajamas during the day, it was easy for me to blend into the crowds of people roaming the halls of the surgical floor. By slipping off my hospital identification bracelet and burying it in my hip pocket, I was able to wander down to the cafeteria for a snack or even to walk Nancy outside to the parking lot.

"Ashpaugh's gone again," was a frequent complaint filed at the second floor nurses' station.

"I think I saw him on the sunroof," offered an aide one afternoon.

"I passed him on Capitol Street this morning when I was coming to work," added another. Finding Bill Ashpaugh soon became the favorite preoccupation of Methodist Hospital personnel. They didn't mind that I usually won the hide-and-seek games, just as long as I stopped by the head nurse's office every four hours for my prescribed assortment of medications.

If I were infamous for my disappearing act, I was equally renowned for my harem of pretty girls. Sisters Kay, Shirley, and Lois rotated shifts, so I was never without a family member in my room. Nancy's presence was so widely accepted that some people thought she was part of the Methodist staff; and then of course, there was mom, forever by my side with just the right words of encouragement and prayer. Her supply of inspirational reading material was endless, and she never left for the evening without marking an article in a magazine or underlining a passage in the Bible for me to ponder when I was alone.

The morning God came into my life—the same day I learned I had cancer—my only regret was I couldn't share my feeling of renewal with Nancy. My sisters, brothers, and parents rejoiced at my spiritual rebirth, but Nancy was left on the outside looking in. She couldn't relate to what was happening to me because she had never been introduced to Jesus Christ.

Her childhood had been vastly different from mine, and hadn't included hours of Bible study, Sunday School, visits from the pastors, tent meetings, and church camp. Saying prayers at night wasn't part of her bedtime ritual, nor was bowing her head before dinner or asking a blessing at family get-togethers. When it came to religion, Nancy and I were at opposite poles. Somehow I had to remedy the situation. The two most important persons in my life—Jesus Christ and Nancy—had to become better acquainted. After all, I planned to spend the rest of my life with both.

When the two Methodist Hospital surgeons relayed the somber news that a cancerous tumor had been removed from my body and there was a possibility of distant spread through my lymph glands and even to my lungs, Nancy was nowhere to be found. She had heard the report out in the hall and had crept away for a few minutes alone before facing the tears in my room. She knew my family would unite around me at such a tragic time and she didn't want to intrude. By the time she returned, her moist eyes carefully powdered and her bright smile back in place, the family had dispersed. All but Lois.

I was propped up on my pillows, clutching my sister's hand and grinning like a man who had received the greatest news of his life rather than his death sentence. Nancy looked bewildered. Hadn't I been told? Didn't I know the prognosis? Was it up to her to explain what the surgeons had spelled out so explicitly in the hall?

"Nancy, it's okay. I'm going to be all right now," I said happily as I reached out to her. She seemed terribly vulnerable, and I knew it was because she cared so much.

She entered the room slowly, totally confused by the joy radiating from Lois and me. For the first time in the entire ordeal of my illness she lost control and allowed tears to spill down her cheeks. I pulled her over to a corner of the bed and let her cry on my shoulder. I wasn't sure I could make her understand or believe what had just happened to me, but I knew I had to try. Maybe someday she could know the joy I was experiencing.

"I'm not going to die, Nancy. I've never been more sure of anything in my whole life. It doesn't matter what the doctors and nurses and all the tests say. I've got Someone looking after me and He's going to heal me. I know you've never believed before, but you can believe this. I've never felt happier, and I want you to be part of it."

She wiped her eyes and dared to look hopeful. She glanced expectantly from me, to Lois, to me again.

"Would you like to meet the Man who's going to make me better?" I asked softly.

"Yes," she answered simply.

"Then close your eyes and pray with me."

I had never been one to express myself very well verbally, yet suddenly the words seemed to well up inside of me and pour out. They were all the right words that had been held in check by my pride for years. They explained exactly how I felt. I asked that God might come into Nancy's life as He had come into mine just minutes before. I prayed that she would be touched by the Holy Spirit and believe that a miracle was possible. I asked that we might all grow together in our faith and might be stronger for carrying the burden He had given us. I even thanked God for the cancer that brought me home to Him.

When I finished, I opened my eyes and looked at Nancy. Her head was still bowed and she was praying in a soft, indistinguishable voice. Her words were uncertain, halting, and strung together with long pauses, but she was reaching out, trying to grab hold. She had never looked more beautiful.

"Bill, I'm not sure I understand all this," she whispered, "But I know you're not going to die. If you say Jesus can heal you, then I believe He can too. I'm not just saying that to be cheerful or because I feel sorry for you. You're going to get better. I'm *sure* of it."

So was I. Suddenly everything in my life seemed to be in harmony. All the loose ends came together. I had a direction, a final destination, and I was no longer traveling alone. Everyone I loved was at my side. Already my new-found faith was spreading out and affecting another life. Nancy was a believer; the seed was planted in her heart and with my help it would grow until it could stand on its own without my support.

In a way, her faith was purer than mine. She was coming to Jesus as a child does, without doubt or question. It was all new to her and she embraced it completely. Whereas my faith had been tested over the years by hypocrites who claimed to be religious but left their spirituality behind in the family pew, she hadn't been exposed to such Sunday-morning Christians. Her faith was totally unshaken and untarnished. Jesus Christ was the answer to what had seemed to be an unsolvable problem.

The doctors, with all their diplomas and degrees, had expressed little hope for my survival. Now suddenly from out of nowhere came the promise of life, happiness, and health. Did she want it? Yes! Was she willing to accept it? You bet! What's more, everywhere she looked she found confirmation of her new beliefs.

My mother up until this time had been too preoccupied with my sickness to take serious note of the pretty girl always posted by my bed or outside my door. I had dated a lot of girls since high school and mom thought of Nancy as merely the most recent. Her impression did an abrupt about-face when Nancy shyly approached her in the hall after we prayed together. Mom was struck by Nancy's strength and determination.

"Mrs. Ashpaugh, I need your help," said Nancy. Mom looked surprised and confused.

"I know Bill's going to be healed. I believe that with all my heart. But that isn't good enough. It doesn't seem right for me to say I'm a Christian just because I want something from Jesus. I owe Him something in return. I want to know Him like you do. I want to learn about the Bible and understand what it says. But where do I begin? Please help me."

Help her? Mom was so touched she wrapped her arms around Nancy and hugged her like a daughter. I watched from my room and marveled at the number of miracles I had witnessed in that one, single day. The morning had begun as the most tragic in my lifetime and yet the evening would end on a glorious note. Only one thing could make it better, and there was still time for that.

I tucked my hospital identification bracelet into my jeans' pocket and walked Nancy downstairs and out into the night. We stopped a few feet from where her girlfriend-turned-chauffeur was waiting to take her home, and under one of those blinding public parking lot lights I kissed her and told her I loved her.

In a sense it was symbolic. At last I wasn't afraid to make a commitment to Nancy in front of the whole world. I wasn't afraid of getting involved; I *wanted* to be involved. Cars driving through the busy Indianapolis intersection tooted and honked their approval. The noise didn't vaguely resemble bells, but it would have to do until I could arrange the real thing. Preferably at a church.

Like falling dominoes, one miracle touched off the next and that one caused another to activate. The immediate change in Nancy was her dogged—and successful—resolution to stop smoking. Before she was saved, she thought cigarettes were necessary accessories for a sophisticated woman. Now she saw them as a weakness that she could live without. After she invited Jesus into her heart, she never smoked again.

She began witnessing to the girls at the restaurant. On her first day back on the job after her week's "vacation," the other waitresses, one by one, offered condolences to her on the prospect of losing her boyfriend. It didn't seem fair, they commiserated, for someone so young to have to die.

"Die?" said Nancy. "Oh, Bill's going to be healed. We're not sure exactly when it will happen, but Jesus is taking care of everything."

Not everyone understood. Some friends thought we

were unrealistic, and they pitied us for our inability to face and accept the cancer. We were criticized for laughing and joking at a time of death. I felt pressured to play the role of the terminally ill patient. It was almost as if people wanted and expected the customary "sick room" environment. I was supposed to cower in my bed; my family was supposed to hover over me; the curtains should be drawn shut, and someone, preferably mom, should be stationed at my side gently coercing me into sipping one more taste of broth or one last spoonful of milk custard.

No way! At the risk of disappointing everyone, my "sick room" was the hub of activity on the surgical floor, my boisterous family had never been happier or closer, and my appetite was downright disgraceful. There was an air of anticipation. The Ashpaughs were expecting a miracle, and they were singing, praying, and preparing for it. Believers were heartily welcomed to participate, and skeptics were invited to wait and see.

A week after I was admitted to the hospital, I was released by a team of reluctant doctors. I respected them and understood their feelings. They thought I was making a big mistake by not agreeing to the extensive surgery they proposed. But they were men of science, doing what their knowledge dictated. I was relying on my faith and was doing what my heart told me to do. Only time would tell which of us was right. In the meantime, I could only pray. And I certainly intended to do a lot of *that!*

"Goin' home for the weekend, Bill?" asked the student nurse who popped in to say hello and found me packing my bags.

"Nope, I'm going home for good," I replied confidently. "You'll never see me here again."

I hurt. As I made my rounds, scooping up my collection of get-well cards on the dresser and my shaving gear in the bathroom, I felt as though I would collapse. The room that had seemed so tiny during my week's occupancy seemed enormous when it came to cleaning it up. Getting dressed took nearly a half hour because I had to sit down frequently to catch my breath.

Once I had stuffed everything that was mine down into my old duffel bag, I took to the halls to say goodbye to the patients and staff who had been so kind to me. I was weak and could barely put one foot in front of the other. My walk, which used to be so spry and confident, was now more like a shuffle. My clothes hung limply on me as an unbecoming reminder of all the weight I had lost. I didn't look like Mr. Indianapolis, and as I inched my way cautiously down the corridor, I didn't feel much like him either.

Nancy arrived, all smiles, to escort me home. Her concern for my appearance was obvious in spite of her cheerfulness. She reached for my luggage, but I brushed her aside.

"Bill, you're tired. For heaven's sakes, let me help you," she urged.

"I can't give in to it, Nancy."

We walked outside to where my car had been parked for nearly a week. Nancy offered to drive, saying she needed the practice since she planned to take her driver's test in just a few days.

It seemed like a legitimate excuse and gave me reason to rest uncomfortably on the passenger side for a few miles. After I regained a bit of strength, I told Nancy to pull over to the shoulder of the road so I could assume duties at the wheel. She started to protest, but stopped. She knew as well as I that I mustn't give up the fight. We were expecting a miracle, weren't we? Any day. Any minute. Our only fear was whether I could endure long enough to receive it.

Chapter 9

HEALING

I went back to the gym long before my doctors gave me clearance. Mom and Nancy objected when I announced, two days into my recuperation, that I was going to work out at Hofmeister's the next morning.

"You can't climb all those stairs," said mom. "You still have stitches in your side."

I knew their fears were justified—I had a few of my own—but worse was the fear I experienced as I felt myself growing weaker every day. It scared me. *Shouldn't I be getting stronger?* I wondered.

When I walked over to Ashpaugh Electric, and tried to catch up on memos and phone calls, I didn't last until noon. I felt so tired and sluggish that Dave finally had to help me home. Short afternoon naps sometimes stretched past dusk, and I was ready to go to bed right after dinner. I decided to fight back the only way I knew how—in the gym, lifting weights. It wouldn't be easy. Getting there was an ordeal, but then I had to face all those buddies who had looked up to me almost as a hero for so many years.

Suddenly I was an object of pity: thin, weak, and without stamina. To make matters worse, my skin had taken on a strange yellow cast. Nancy and I had spent hours basking in the sun at Hillside Beach in Noblesville, but it had done no good. The sickly yellow neither faded nor was covered by a healthy tan. I heard people whisper that I was jaundiced; that my color was "cancer yellow."

Before I went into the hospital, all the talk in the gym had revolved around the upcoming Mr. Indiana contest. As runner-up the year before, I was favored to win it all. This was to be "Bill's year," according to local body-building authorities. I had worked hard for it and I deserved it. But "Bill's year" ended prematurely the day I walked back into the gym after the surgery.

Even the most sympathetic friend couldn't conceal his amazement at my appearance. I was haggard-looking—my face was thin; my features, sharp and gaunt. Even my normally snug-fitting gym trunks hung loosely around my waist. I greeted the guys warmly and tried to put them at their ease. Some tried too hard to be kind and casual, while others found it difficult to even look at me.

"I'm starting over," I said honestly. "I'm back at square one again. I don't want anyone feeling sorry for me. I'm going to whip this thing. I'm going to be back on top. I might even win Mr. Indiana after all. Don't count me out yet!"

I started with the smallest set of dumbbells and lifted them slowly over my head, straight out in front of me, open wide at my sides, then down to my hips. *One-two-three-four.* Every movement caused a tugging sensation around my sutures. Again: *one-two-three-four.* My muscles felt taut and unused as I gasped for breath. *One-two-three-four.*

The walls of mirrors reflected a lean, sallow man quivering under the stress of the simplest warm-up exercise. I clamped my eyes closed to shut out the view. I was determined to do twenty-five lifts today and another fifty tomorrow. Another deep breath: *one-two-three-four. How it hurt!*

Each subsequent visit to the gym was easier. The guys accepted my presence and the fact I was no longer a competitor. They understood that I was a beginner again, slowly building up from an abbreviated workout routine to a more moderate schedule. Sheer determination caused me to regain a little of my strength, but everyone knew my progress was far below normal. I refused to give in, pushing myself to lift a little more, stretch a little farther, fight a little harder.

I became very good at reading other people's eyes and gauging my decline by their reactions. It's hard to be publicly pitied, yet my only alternative was to become a recluse and putter around the family farm. That wasn't my style. I wanted to be out with people, witnessing to them and telling them about the miracle that was going to heal me. Any day now. Any minute. Just wait and see.

Even more difficult than entering the gym for the first time after surgery was stopping by the neighborhood hamburger haven and saying hello to all the gang that congregated there. When I won the Mr. Indianapolis contest, I had advanced to semi-celebrity status around Noblesville and was treated like royalty—Hoosier style. Gathering place for all my hometown pals was Jim Dandy's restaurant, where the manager, waitresses, and clientele knew Bill Ashpaugh as the local boy who had made good.

Now I was deposed, stripped of my strength, and left a shell of my former self. I felt like a paper tiger. All my trophies only served as cold, tarnished reminders of what I used to be. The self-confident mass of muscle who had once sauntered around town and held court at "his" table had been replaced by a feather-weight.

But, in many ways, the new Bill Ashpaugh was a better person than the old one had been. My false pride was gone and I had my priorities in order. I was more content, less self-centered, and happier than I had ever been before.

Still, as I witnessed to people and told them that God was going to heal me, I could read the doubt in their eyes. I couldn't really blame them. I certainly didn't *look* like a man who was being touched by the hand of God. Yet, I had to keep my faith, continue smiling, never let that first doubt cause my trust in Jesus to waver. I had to believe that my body was rejecting the cancer that had staked a claim in it, and that I was getting stronger every day. It wasn't easy.

"Nancy, I can't go in there," I said, as we pulled into the parking lot at Jim Dandy's restaurant. I recognized all the cars and pickup trucks of my friends. Most of them hadn't seen me since my surgery, but they knew what the doctors had told me. Bad news travels fast in a small town.

"Of course you can," said Nancy. "We're going to march in there just like we always have, say hello to everyone, sit at our usual table and you're going to joke and goof around with all the guys. If we act like we're beaten, how can we hope to win?"

She was right, of course. We marched in—actually *she* marched and I brought up the rear—and greeted everyone as if nothing had happened. The reception we were given was cool and restrained. Whereas I had always before been able to count on one of the teen-age waitresses to bustle over immediately and take our order, this time twenty minutes passed before we were approached. I knew the waitress well, had watched her grow up, and had taught her big brother to lift weights, but today she seemed a stranger. She couldn't look me in the eye. She mumbled a greeting and, once we had ordered, turned on her heels and practically ran away.

To combat the tension my presence seemed to elicit, Nancy and I laughed, joked, and managed to have a good time. We had every reason to be happy—we were expecting a miracle. How I wished others could share our anticipation. It was up to me to make them believe.

I began to witness at every opportunity. Word that Bill Ashpaugh was willing to give his testimony spread among local church groups. *Willing?* I felt *driven* to tell my story. I wasn't a polished public speaker, but I found I was most effective if I didn't prepare my talk in advance, instead letting the Spirit move in me. I believed so strongly in what I was saying that I never felt nervous. I talked honestly about my sport, my experience with drugs, my cancer, and my healing.

"It's coming," I told group after group. "Any day. Any minute."

For every speech I gave, some member of my family gave two. My fight with cancer and my spiritual rebirth had affected my sisters, brothers, and parents. They also felt led to witness, tell my story, and explain how my renewal of faith had revived and strengthened their own beliefs.

If the Lord was at work in our lives, so was the devil. He popped up when I least expected him. One afternoon as I drove my usual route through Indianapolis on my way home from Hofmeister's, I was halted by a red light.

Hmmm, when did they put a traffic signal here? I wondered. Then I looked to my left and saw I had stopped in front of the largest funeral home in the city. A casket was being carried out to a waiting caravan of cars marked with small black flags. Usually, I would merely have felt reverent, but under the circumstances, I was overcome with fear. No one was with me to squeeze my hand, offer assurances, or simply change the subject. I said a silent prayer and drove on.

I was plagued by nightmares about my own death. I could see Nancy crying and my brothers-in-law comforting my sisters. The scene was always the same—the Lakeview Wesleyan Church, filled with arrangements of fall flowers, and with an overflow congregation and a full choir singing from the loft. I'd wake up, damp with perspiration, shaking from the reality of it.

The seed of this nightmare had apparently been planted by a friend, a former classmate, when he approached me in all seriousness and said he'd be pleased—honored, in fact—to be one of my pallbearers. I stared at him in disbelief. How could anyone *think* such a thing, let alone say it!

"I'm not going to die," I answered. "Jesus is going to heal me. Why can't anyone believe that?"

I was losing weight daily. Mom finally hid the bathroom scales so I wouldn't be aware of how rapidly the pounds were peeling off my body.

She continued to minister to me in other quiet, gentle ways. She'd suggest that I stretch out on the living room sofa while she put dinner on the table, and, when I followed her advice, I'd find an open Bible on the coffee table with an appropriate passage underlined in red. Magazine articles about divine healing would somehow find their way to the small table by my bed. The red pen was the giveaway—it was the same one she used to jot down her grocery list.

Nancy was equally supportive, but no one could accuse her of being the strong, silent type. She bubbled with enthusiasm for her new-found faith and never doubted for a minute that I would be healed. Her friends cautioned her that I was too old for her. After they learned of my cancer, they counseled her to think twice before getting seriously involved with me. When I finally worked up the courage to ask her to marry me, it was a conditional proposal.

"Nancy, if everything goes all right, will you marry me?" I asked sheepishly. Her answer came in the form of a kiss and a wonderful smile that erased all my doubts. Still, we didn't set an exact date, but decided sometime in the fall would be best—after I had received my miracle. In anticipation of life together, we began shopping for a mobile home. While most of Noblesville and Westfield was prophesying my death, Nancy and I were scouring the countryside for just the right site for our home on wheels and weighing the pros and cons of Early American *vs.* Danish Modern decor.

"Sure you want to go through with this?" I'd ask from time to time.

"I'm sure," she always answered.

Two weeks had passed since my release from the hospital. Although my spiritual being was growing stronger every day, I continued to deteriorate physically. In spite of all my efforts in the gym, I was still weak and it took every bit of stamina I could muster to endure a short workout. I couldn't put in a full day at the office, and I found myself falling asleep earlier every night and waking up later every morning. By the time I was due to see Dr. Gabrielsen to have my stitches removed, I weighed less than I had as a teen-ager training out in the old chicken shed.

"Won't you reconsider and let us take you back into surgery, Bill?"

"You won't have to. I'm going to be healed. Jesus is going to take care of everything."

I was ready for my miracle, but it didn't seem ready for me. I prayed; I studied the Bible; I witnessed; I waited. Nothing happened. Another two weeks went by.

Methodist Hospital called and reminded me of my agreement to come back for a dye test. It was a simple procedure, the nurse explained, but it would take most of the day. Dye would be injected into my hands and feet and any recurrence of cancer would be detected by x-rays. Just a day or two after the test the doctor would be able to tell me if I still had cancer in my body, where it was, and how fast it was spreading. Could she schedule the test for the following Tuesday? I agreed. It was Friday, and I had exactly three days for my miracle to take place.

"Lord, I'm Your servant. I want to work for You, speak for You, and win souls for You. But if that isn't Your plan, I understand. I accept Your will. I surrender to You."

Saturday came and went. No miracle. On Sunday morning I woke up early and decided to attend the first service at church. Dad was away on a fishing trip in Canada and was due back that afternoon. Mom was in the kitchen cooking something special for his welcome-home dinner, so I went off by myself. I arrived a little late, and in order not to disturb the rest of the congregation, I found a seat in the back. A young girl was giving a reading from 1 Samuel:

> Then said David to the Philistine, Thou comest to me with a sword, and with a spear, and with a shield: but I come to thee in the name of the Lord of hosts, the God of the armies of Israel, whom thou hast defied.
>
> This day will the Lord deliver thee into mine hand; and I will smite thee, and take thine head from thee; and I will give the carcases of the host of the Philistines this day unto the fowls of the air, and to the wild beasts of the earth; that all the earth may know that there is a God in Israel. (1 Sam. 17:45-46.)

The words penetrated my mind, bouncing around in my head. I had always loved that portion of the Old Testament because it was the story of strength, of good conquering evil in spite of obvious odds. It was the classic tale of the underdog overpowering the giant. I had clung to it when I was a little boy, smaller than all my friends. David had been my hero and I had never tired of hearing of his victory. But today the words had special meaning. It was as if the passages were directed especially to me. There was a message that was meant for my ears alone.

Suddenly I was aware of a second voice overriding that of the young girl in the pulpit. It was what I had waited to hear for thirty days.

"Tonight, son, you're going to be healed."

I felt like the keeper of a wonderful secret that I couldn't share with anyone. I couldn't tell my pastor—he was the one who had been so willing to bundle me off to heaven when I was in the hospital. I couldn't tell the people seated around me. What good would it do? I had been telling them for weeks that I would be healed and no one believed me.

I hurried home and found mom putting the finishing touches on an enormous Sunday dinner. I hugged her until she yelped that she couldn't breathe.

"God spoke to me in church, mom. It's finally happened. He's going to heal me tonight!"

Although I had only been awake for a few hours, I was overcome with sleepiness. I couldn't eat any of mom's dinner, but instead, excused myself and went upstairs to my room. I slept soundly all afternoon. When I woke up at five, I knew exactly what I was supposed to do. First, I went to the phone and called my sisters, brothers, and friends who had prayed for so many weeks for this miracle. The last one on my list was the most important—Nancy.

"Will you go to a meeting with me tonight?" I asked. "I'm going to be healed. It's what we've been waiting for."

It was the twenty-first of June and all the churches in our area had banded together to sponsor a week-long Youth for Christ tent meeting just west of Noblesville on State Road 38. I knew that was where I was supposed to go that evening at seven o'clock.

I wasn't on the program. I hadn't been asked to speak. But I had a special invitation from the Host. *Yes, Lord, I'll be there,* I thought as I put on my best coat and tie. I drove down to Indianapolis and picked up Nancy, then stopped by to gather up my parents, sisters, and brothers. They were as much a part of this miracle as I was.

When we arrived at the tent, we claimed a row of folding chairs for our little delegation. Hundreds of people had turned out for the opening session, and I suddenly realized I had no idea exactly *how* I was going to be healed. Surely I would have to go forward to the altar, but I knew this particular Youth for Christ group didn't include a healing segment or conclude with an altar call. I decided to leave such details to the Master. Midway through the program, He solved the problem.

"Friends, I see we have a special guest with us tonight," said the tent leader. "Could I ask Bill Ashpaugh, our own Mr. Indianapolis, to come forward and say a few words to all the young people?"

Thank you, Lord, I thought as I made my way across the rows of chairs and down the long aisle to the speaker's podium. I still didn't know what I should say, but I trusted Jesus to give me the words. He hadn't failed me yet.

"I think you all know that I was recently diagnosed as having cancer," I began simply. "Some people might think that's the worst thing that could happen to a guy. But for me, it's been the best. It took cancer to bring me back to the Lord. I've given my life to Jesus Christ, and in return, I believe He is going to heal me here tonight."

I could feel the apprehension in the air and could hear the people shift uncomfortably in their squeaky wooden chairs. There were a lot of unbelievers out there, but God had said this was the place of my miracle and I put my trust in Him.

"I've never seen anybody healed before, and maybe you haven't either. But won't you help me? Won't you come forward and pray for me?"

I turned my back to the congregation and walked up to the altar. I could hear people getting out of their seats and quietly making their way up the grassy aisle to form an arc behind me. I got down on my knees and bowed my head.

We prayed long and hard in silence. Nothing happened. Slowly, one by one, the people at the altar slipped away and went back to their chairs. I felt dizzy and weak, but I kept praying. I spoke to God like a child would, asking him to help me, cure me, heal me. Still nothing happened. I was the only one left at the altar—a completely humbled mound of humanity hunched in prayer under a tattered khaki tent in the middle of an Indiana cornfield. But where was Jesus? He promised He'd be there.

I suddenly remembered a Scripture passage from the New Testament. I had never tried to memorize it, yet I could see it written in front of me, word for word. It seemed to hold a special message for me. I repeated it over and over to myself.

> And when they could not come nigh unto him for the press, they uncovered the roof where he was: and when they had broken it up, they let down the bed wherein the sick of the palsy lay.
>
> When Jesus saw their faith, he said unto the sick of the palsy, Son, thy sins be forgiven thee.
>
> I say unto thee, Arise, and take up thy bed, and go thy way into thine house. (Mark 2:4-5, 11)

Faith. It all came down to pure, unquestioned faith. I needed to believe in God's power so completely that I could claim my healing even before it was manifested. No doubts, no fears. I needed to assume that God's will—the desire to cleanse my body of disease—had been done. Why didn't I understand this before? While I was waiting for Jesus to act, He was waiting for me to prove my faith.

I looked straight up and raised both hands over my head and toward the heavens. I could hardly straighten my arms out. It was as if I were lifting a 100-pound dumbbell in each hand. The congregation sat in total silence, watching.

"Thank you, Jesus, for taking this cancer from my body," I said.

As soon as the words were out of my mouth I felt overcome with a warm feeling. The source of the heat was my lower abdomen, swirling and churning upward. I fell to the ground, drained of what little strength I had had. A man from the audience came forward and helped lift me up. I walked back and forth down the aisle clutching hands and hugging shoulders.

"I'm healed. I really believe I'm healed," I said joyfully. I could see the Ashpaugh delegation, including Nancy, laughing, crying, and squeezing each other. I fell into their arms and let them lead me out into the night.

First thing Tuesday morning I was up and driving south on the interstate headed for Methodist Hospital. I'm no singer, but I had my radio blasting and I was bellowing along in off-key harmony. *Lord, it's great to be alive,* I thought.

I felt good, my energy level was up and I was actually looking forward to the long, arduous dye test that was scheduled for me. A month before I had driven the same route in pain and fear. Today I felt *clean,* free of drugs, free of foolish aspirations, and free of cancer. This test would prove the victory over disease. I already knew what the results would be.

"Hey, Ashpaugh's back!"

"Hi, Bill!"

I was greeted by doctors, nurses, and staffers as though I were a long-lost buddy. They were my friends, great people who had shared the most difficult moments of my life with me. Now I wanted them to be a part of the victory—the happy ending. I wanted the whole world to know about my healing.

"Are you going to put me to sleep?" I asked, as I stretched out on an examining table.

"Nope, not this time," the nurse replied.

"Good, then I can talk while you're working on me, right?"

"Right."

Under the watchful eye of a radiologist, dye was pumped through tiny punctures in my feet to circulate throughout my body. After a certain amount of time had elapsed, x-rays were taken.

"Do you go to church?" I asked a somewhat surprised doctor and his assistant.

"Sure, we go to church," answered the nurse.

"Well, I went to a service Sunday night and I was healed. You aren't going to find any cancer in me today. Miracles are possible if only you believe hard enough."

They glanced uncomfortably at each other and then at me. Eyebrows were raised and little smiles crossed their faces. It was obvious to them that poor Bill Ashpaugh was suffering from delusions. *Terminal illness will do that to a person,* their expressions seemed to say.

When the test was finally over, I was instructed to go home and take it easy for the rest of the day. I would be able to get the doctor's full report on the results by calling his office after 1 P.M. the next day. I followed the directive *almost* to the letter: I did go home and take it easy, but after a two-hour workout at the gym. I felt great!

On Wednesday, promptly at 1 P.M. , I gathered mom,

dad, Nancy, and the rest of the family around the phone to make that all-important call. Excited, nervous, confident, and frightened, I attempted to dial the number. Five times I was greeted by that persistent, grinding busy signal. On the sixth try I reached the surgeon's office.

"This is Bill Ashpaugh, and I'm calling to find out the results of the lymphangiogram you did yesterday."

A long pause followed as we waited for his nurse to pull my file. I heard papers being shuffled and finally the words: "Here it is." Reaching out for Nancy, I shut my eyes and tightened my grip on the telephone.

"Let's see," began the doctor, scanning the report. "It says here that twenty-four-hour lymphangiogram films show the lymph nodes to be of normal size, shape, and distribution. There are no filling defects to suggest the presence of malignant deposits, nor is there any evidence of lymphoma. We saw a few minor filling defects in the pelvic region, but they were bilateral and can be ascribed to the inflammatory deposits that are almost constantly present."

"Doc, hold it, please," I interrupted. "I don't understand all those words. Just tell me straight. Did the test show any cancer?"

"No, Bill, it didn't."

It wasn't necessary to use words to relay the message to Nancy or my family. My smiles and tears told them emphatically that the news was good. Our prayers had been answered. With God's help we had fought a battle against almost impossible odds and we had won. I wanted to tell the whole world the story of my miracle, but I would start at home, in Noblesville. It was a beginning. I grabbed Nancy's hand and ran out to the car.

"Let's go down to Jim Dandy's," I said, depositing her on the passenger side and then running around to slip in beside her.

"You're hungry?" she asked incredulously.

"No, but there are a few people in this town who need to hear about the results of that test. Maybe then they'll be convinced that Jesus can heal."

I'm not sure I won any souls that day, but we certainly caused a few heads to turn and a few folks to re-examine their convictions that miracles aren't a part of the twentieth century. I felt *alive* and I looked like I could take on the world and win. My color was normal and my walk was light. My face and body radiated health and energy. I was on my way back. Better than ever.

We announced our wedding date shortly after our miracle was confirmed: September 13 at Lakeview Wesleyan Church. I suggested a simple ceremony with only our families and a few close friends attending. Nancy wouldn't hear of it. She wanted all the trimmings, and her argument was a good one.

"This should be a celebration of life," she said. "Most people didn't expect to see you in September, and they certainly didn't expect to see you getting married! Our ceremony will symbolize what God can do when people believe in Him."

So, a big wedding it would be. Very big. Sometimes I wonder if Nancy didn't consult Cecil B. DeMille on some of the arrangements. We didn't exactly have a cast of thousands, but we did have a matron of honor, a best man, and an abundance of bridesmaids, groomsmen, ushers, flower girls, ring bearers, cake and punch servers. Everyone wanted to help celebrate our victory and we welcomed their enthusiasm.

The end result was a beautiful spiritual happening which was staged in the same location as the funeral I had seen in my dreams. Great bunches of fall flowers decorated the sanctuary, a choir sang from the loft, and an overflow congregation crowded into the pews and lined the side aisles. But the mood was one of joy.

Surely there were never two happier people than Mr.
and Mrs. Bill Ashpaugh as they headed south to the
Smoky Mountains for their honeymoon. (The fact they
only got as far as Cincinnati is immaterial, right?)

We took a full week off from work to become accus-
tomed to being a "we" instead of an "I" and an "us"
instead of a "me." Then it was back to the normal
routine again of working and working out. I had one final
battle to fight—I was going to go after the Mr. Indiana
title in spite of all the weeks of training I missed during
my sickness. I was at a disadvantage, because I had
been completely off steroids for five months and any
positive effects they might have had on my physique
were long since gone. I would enter this contest clean.

I had about sixty days to formulate and carry out a
crash training program. Nancy helped, not only by cooking the high-protein meals I needed, but by never complaining about the fact that her bridegroom spent most of
his time in the gym. She understood this was the dream
I had held onto since I was a little kid, so she made it her
dream too. With that kind of support, how could I possibly fail?

The contest was set for Whiting, Indiana, in
November, with fourteen guys fighting for the right to
add "Mr. Indiana"—the big one—to their lists of honors.
The title meant different things to different athletes.
Some saw it as a stepping stone to the national
contests—Mr. America, Mr. USA. Others hoped to turn
professional and make a living traveling around the
country giving shows and talks, or opening a gym of
their own. A few probably saw the contest as a launching pad to a final destination of Hollywood.

As for me, my purpose for entering seemed to be
unique. I knew kids need heroes and they're more willing to listen to what a guy says if they respect what
he's done. I had an important message I wanted to take

to young people, and I figured they would give me their attention more readily if they were just a little in awe of me. I saw the Mr. Indiana title as an entrance, a means to an end.

With my goal set, I went after it with all the determination of a man possessed. My body weight climbed, and so did my strength. I ran, I swam, I rowed, and I lifted to get into shape. When the night of the contest finally came, I not only was back to my pre-cancer form, I was better. I had done it with God's help and *without* any assistance from a bottle of little blue pills.

The reward for our efforts—Jesus' and mine—came in the form of a five-foot-tall trophy and a title most people thought I could never achieve. But the victory also carried a responsibility. I had my entrance . . . now what was I going to do with it?

Chapter 10

FITNESS AND WITNESS

"We've got a full house," the principal said, welcoming me backstage with a bone-crushing handshake. *Ouch.* One of the drawbacks of being known for your strength is that everyone you meet feels obligated to prove he has something in common with you. I've met more than my share of Herculeses and Charles Atlases.

Actually, the principal's words caused me more pain than did his grip. I was nervous, and knowing we had a capacity crowd on hand—I had already peeked through the slit in the curtains twice—didn't help. What group was this anyway? An athletic banquet? A convocation? A scout meeting? A church fellowship? Not that it mattered. The challenge was familiar: I was to get their attention; wow 'em; then tell my story and hope they would hear . . . *really* hear its message.

* * *

During those long weeks after my release from Methodist Hospital, as I waited for something, *anything,* to happen, I toyed with the idea of giving up bodybuilding completely. After all, it *is* a sport that glorifies the body and puts a lot of emphasis on physical perfection. *Isn't it wrong for a dedicated Christian to spend hours every day trying to improve his appearance?* I wondered.

As much as I enjoyed the challenge of competing, the healthy environment of a gym, and the friendships that sprout there, I was willing to put it all behind me. Even after I was healed I weighed the pros and cons of continuing in my sport. If only I could know what was right, what *He* had in mind for me . . .

Maybe I'm supposed to witness to other athletes, I thought. I could train side by side with them and tell them the dangers of drugs and the value of getting your head together. I could explain about my cancer and the miracle that healed me.

It sounded good, but I knew it wouldn't work. Guys in a gym don't want to be preached to or made to feel they're doing something wrong. Usually they work out with weights to unwind and forget the pressures of the world outside. They certainly don't want some prophet in gym trunks warning them to shape up spiritually as well as physically.

In spite of mom's dream of my entering the ministry, I still couldn't see myself living the admirable, but structured, life of a pastor. I'm too much of a maverick—not a great reader, deep thinker, or polished speaker—just a good ol' country boy. I say what's on my mind and in my heart. A clerical collar would never fit comfortably on this overgrown neck of mine.

So what will it be, Lord? I asked time and time again. Where can I help most? What people can I reach for You with my story? As usual, the answer was right in front of me all the time. I only needed to look.

* * *

"Thanks for coming, Bill," the athletic director said, extending a hand that seemed determined to destroy the feeling in mine. Oh well, thank goodness I'm left-handed. It was awards night at a local high school and I had been invited to give the program.

Though it had been several weeks since my healing, I was still wrestling with the idea of retiring from competitive bodybuilding. In the meantime, I had been giving talks to church fellowship groups in the area, telling them about my experience with cancer and how God had made all the difference in my life.

"We've got a tough audience out there for you," continued the coach apologetically. "It's a packed house, and the kids are rowdy. Last year the speaker had to quit halfway through because the boys got restless and were throwing spitballs."

His words waved like a red flag in front of me. No one loves a challenge more than I do, even when it comes from a group of teen-age kids who have left their manners at home. When I spoke, they were going to listen and listen good.

"I guarantee they won't be throwing any spitballs tonight," I answered firmly.

After dinner and the presentation of athletic awards, the emcee announced he was turning over the program to me. The squeaking of chairs and undercurrents of conversation stopped abruptly when the auditorium went totally dark. Two spotlights snapped on simultaneously and focused their strong white beams on the stage where I stood in trunks and a tank top. The combination of spotlights and silence made a dramatic scene.

As I began my posing routine, the strains of a popular instrumental song familiar to all the kids filtered in through the public address system. Slowly I moved from one position to the next, letting the rhythm guide me. Since my audience was made up of athletes who were especially appreciative of strength, I emphasized poses that showed the greatest muscularity. The routine lasted four minutes, a full minute longer than AAU-sponsored contests' recommended time. Still, I never lost the kids' attention. When the auditorium went dark again, there was no nervous rustling or bored chatter. The stage lights came up and I was ready to dip into my bag of tricks and wow 'em.

"Ever wondered what the telephone company does with all its old Indianapolis directories?" I asked. "Well, they used to pay to have them shredded, but now they give them to me instead. I work for free."

Someone backstage handed me the four-inch-thick book of yellow pages. There were a few *ooohs* and *aahhs* and a smattering of applause as I promptly ripped it in two.

"How many of you have ever seen a steel bar like this?" I asked, producing a five-eighths-inch solid steel rod. "Road crews use them to build highways. But I like to have a little fun with them. Now I'm probably not the only guy in the world who can bend this bar with his hands, but I bet there aren't many guys who can bend it with their teeth."

The audience was beginning to get involved. What's the old expression—*you could have heard a pin drop?* I decided to play their anticipation and excitement for all they were worth.

"Could I have a towel, please?" I looked offstage where the athletic director gave me a wink and a terry cloth gym towel. "I wouldn't recommend that any of you guys try this. A beginner could do a lot of damage to himself. Remember, I've been in training for years."

Dramatically, I mopped my head of perspiration— more from the hot spotlights than from tension—then I wrapped the rod in the towel and put the middle of it in my mouth. After a couple of false starts to increase the tension, I bent the bar double with a mighty grunt of power. A great burst of applause erupted. But I wasn't done yet. Not by a long shot.

"All you guys who call yourselves athletes are familiar

with this, right?'' I asked, holding up a rubber hot-water bottle. ''This is what your coach packs with ice when you sprain your ankle or your trainer fills with hot water when you've got a charley horse. But I've found another use for it. I like to blow it up until it bursts. Now, just like bending the steel rod, this can be dangerous. I'm going to ask all of you fellows sitting in the first couple of rows to move back, and I'd like total silence from everyone else because this takes a lot of concentration. Could I have my towel back, please?''

With a great flourish, the towel was tied around my eyes to protect them from rubber fragments. *Too bad I can't have a drum roll,* I thought, as I began huffing and puffing. The tension grew as the bottle expanded. I heard a few nervous sighs and some equally nervous *''Shhhhhs''* as the bottle ballooned forth, stretched taut. Finally it exploded, and so did the audience. The kids were clapping and stomping and so were their parents.

''One more trick?'' I asked the audience.

''Yes!'' was the reply in unison.

''Okay, but I'm going to need your help on this one. Could I have four volunteers? I want the biggest, strongest guys in the house to come up on stage with me. Don't be shy; give me the best you got,'' I challenged.

Wow, they grow 'em big in this part of Indiana, I decided as four good-natured ''giants'' strode across the stage. We shook hands. Ouch, I might have known—it was the old Charles Atlas grip again, times four.

''I think I'm going to need a *couple* of towels for this one,'' I joked to my ''assistant,'' the friendly athletic director. He went scurrying off in the direction of the showers. When he returned with the towels, we wrapped each of my upper arms in fabric and tied separate pieces of heavy rope around my right and left biceps.

Then I gripped my lower right arm with my left hand and my left arm with my right hand.

"Ready, guys?" I asked.

"Ready."

"Okay, I want two of you on each side, and when I say 'go,' you start pulling on the ropes with all your might. Try to break my grip on my arms if you can. I'll try to hang on to a count of ten. Audience, will you count for us?"

Just as I thought, they were more than willing to get involved in the action. I took an exaggerated deep breath and said, "Go!"

The four men pulled and tugged as the audience began the countdown. "Count faster!" I urged through clenched teeth.

"Seven, eight, nine . . . ten!" I let go and so did the applause. I shook all my assistants' hands—I'm a glutton for punishment—and slipped into my warm-up suit. Now that I had everyone's attention, I could get down to business. We could discuss the *real* reason I was there. Suddenly none of the school administrators were worried about spitballs.

"How many of you guys are athletes?" I asked. As I had expected, almost every hand belonging to a guy under eighteen shot up. "Okay, how many of you are Christians?" There was a pause, a few more hands stretched up, a few came down, but most were stalled uncertainly in mid-air.

"Well, I think all athletes should be Christians and all Christians should be athletes. Why? Because Christians and athletes have something in common—they have to have discipline. You know, in order to be tops in your sport you have to be physically and mentally disciplined. To be a good Christian you have to be spiritually disciplined. To be a well-rounded person you should be disciplined in all three ways—mentally, physically, and spiritually. That's the ultimate goal.''

I told them about my early years of training for weight lifting, when my desire to win was so great that it caused me to lose touch with more important goals. I explained how I came to depend on pills—steroids—to make me bigger, stronger, faster. I told them how the pills helped me win trophies and ribbons and titles that suddenly lost their meaning when that ugly, painful tumor appeared in my body.

''Trophies aren't much help when you're lying in a hospital bed and the people you love best are standing around you crying because they think you're going to die.''

The audience was totally attentive as I recounted my surgery and my decision to go home and wait for God to heal me. I described my appearance, my color, and my weight loss.

'''It happened, guys. I'm here, standing in front of you as living proof of what Jesus can do when He comes into your lives. So don't sell out to drugs or any other shortcut to success. There's a better way. Stay clean, train hard, and keep in touch with the One who has ultimate power and strength. Don't be shy about being a Christian. Don't be ashamed that you believe. Stand up and be counted. I did, and I've never been sorry.''

I'm not sure which was the most gratifying—the standing ovation, the parents and kids who crowded on the stage to shake my hand, or what the principal said as he walked me out to the car.

''You don't know how much good you have done here tonight, Bill. Those kids know what you're talking about. They've been exposed to the drugs and they've heard all the great things the pills and injections are supposed to do for athletes. We can talk to them, warn them, preach to them, even threaten them, but they really need to hear it from someone like you. Tonight they finally got the message. They *really* listened."

As I drove home to Nancy that night, I felt jubilant. Maybe this was to be my niche. Maybe I was to carry God's Word to young athletes who could identify with me, hear my story, and benefit from it. Mom might have been right after all—the Lord had a very special ministry in mind for me, one in which the "minister" wears a warm-up suit instead of a collar and carries a telephone book instead of a Bible. Hopefully, my approach might touch lives, gather souls, and deliver them into the care of the Lord and the guidance of a church. Yes, such a ministry suited me. I was comfortable with it. It allowed me to be myself.

More doors opened to me when I added the Mr. Indiana title to my list of credentials. My ministry expanded beyond high school gyms and even outside the Hoosier state. One of the most difficult assignments the Lord gave me came as a result of an invitation from Cleveland Browns' football star Bill Glass. He was gathering together a group of Christian athletes to tour several prisons around the country to minister to inmates. The audiences would be tough, he explained. Did I want to tackle them?

"Sure," I replied, having no idea what I as getting myself into. As usual, this country boy had a lot to learn.

The basic format for each prison visit would be the same. First, the inmates would be invited—never required—to attend our show. The purpose would be purely to provide entertainment, and the acts would vary according to the athletes on the bill. A well-known basketball player might get things moving by singing and strumming a guitar, a football star might follow and play jazz piano, a karate expert might demolish watermelons and stacks of two-by-four planks, or I might do a weight-lifting-bodybuilding routine. Our "stage" would often be a semi-trailer, pulled into the middle of the prison campus. Inmates, most of them exhibiting a "show-me" attitude, would wander in lack-adaisically and fill up the bleachers. No Christian testimony would be given during the entertainment, but the athletes always invited the audience to return that evening for some serious talk.

"You've got to challenge these guys," explained Bill Glass. "If you don't, they won't come back at night."

It wasn't easy. I soon learned that some of our best athletes are behind bars. I saw a retired superstar from the Boston Celtics take on an inmate in a one-on-one game—the pro lost. Weight lifting is especially popular with prisoners because it's a means of survival. They know if they can get big and strong enough, other prisoners won't pick on them.

In Seattle, I met a former Mr. Oakland who had just robbed a bank and was behind bars. He had found it much easier to train in prison than on the "outside." The equipment was the best, the drugs were plentiful, and, "Besides," he said, "in prison there's really nothing better to pass the time."

Consequently, a lot of inmates with whom I had contact could do everything I could do or more. I found it necessary to "prove" myself to my audience night after night.

An experience at a prison somewhere in Pennsylvania was a near-disaster and almost sent me packing back to Noblesville. I knew Bill Glass was watching me carefully to see how "the new kid" handled a difficult audience, and I was determined to succeed.

But I hadn't counted on the presence of a heckler. This guy sat right in front—a real motor-mouth—and spouted a non-stop string of obscenities throughout my program. He had a smart reply for everything I said, he ridiculed each feat of strength, and he was slowly causing the audience to turn against me and join him in his cruel commentary on my performance.

I felt myself losing control, but I decided to end my show as planned, with the water bottle trick. The towel was tied around my eyes for protection, I gulped a deep breath of air and began to blow into the bottle. Maybe because the crowd had rattled me, I couldn't get the bottle to burst. With every breath the jeers increased, as more and more inmates joined in the attempt to devastate me. Finally, just as the bottle was inflated to what must have been near-bursting, I got mad. Fighting mad. I ripped off the towel and was surprised to see the entire audience had moved back about thirty feet. They were afraid of the hot water bottle!

I glared at my persistent heckler and said, "One more word, buddy, and I'm going to burst this thing right in your face."

"Oh no, brother, don't do that! You're okay. I'll lay off," he said. And he did.

That night's program was one of the best I have ever given. The audience became quiet, courteous, and receptive—ready to listen to my story. But I didn't have time to bask in my success after the show—the next night would mean another prison, a new audience, and a fresh challenge.

Talking to individual inmates was much easier than talking to a group of them gathered together, I learned. Bill Glass had suggested that we fan out at each prison and socialize with as many residents as we could, rather than separating ourselves into "them" and "us" forces. I'd usually start by visiting the prison gym and pumping iron for a while. Then I'd latch onto a couple of inmates as lunch companions. Except for the guard following me with a sawed-off shotgun, I could have been mistaken for one of the boys.

I found that on a person-to-person basis, most of the guys aren't very different from people on the outside.

They like to talk about the same things as every other "typical" American male—girls, sports, music, home, and family. They like rubbing elbows with athletes, especially those who have done well in their sport, because it makes them feel important. Being "somebody" is very much a goal, and they achieve it either by their own talents or by associating with "winners." They looked on us visiting athletes with a certain amount of awe and vied for an opportunity to get close to us, talk to us, eat with us, and (hopefully) to pray with us.

Try as I might, I was never able to distinguish particular types of offenders. Although the prisoners and I didn't often discuss specific reasons why they were in jail, at the end of the day I might learn from prison officials that the guy with whom I ate lunch was serving a life sentence for murder. Or the fellow who helped me pump up before the show was a confessed rapist. Their friendly, low-key manners never gave away their history of violence. Theirs were different kinds of lives, to which I had never before been exposed. I was a long, long way from Westfield, Indiana!

At a San Francisco prison I was taken to the maximum security cellblock to perform for thirty solitary residents, among them Sirhan Sirhan, Robert Kennedy's killer.

A guard told me that one of the men had committed murder only two days before. During an evening movie, when the lights were low, the inmate walked up to another prisoner in the front row and stabbed him. When the victim fell and rolled over, revealing his face, the killer uttered a surprised: "Sorry, buddy, I thought you were somebody else." A life snuffed out, and all the person responsible could say was, "Sorry, buddy."

I grew up a lot during our tour of duty in the jails and prisons. It was rewarding work, but often discouraging.

Some of the men we met seemed honestly open to our message. But we could only stay such a short time . . .

I often wondered if the little taste of Jesus that we brought in during our brief visit was enough to sustain them and fortify them against the negative forces of their surroundings. We were fighting the odds since, according to experts' figures, most prisons have an eighty percent return rate. I could only hope and pray our efforts brought about some small bit of success.

Although the inmates regarded us as the "lucky" ones who could walk out of the cells at the end of a long day, we also paid a price for being there. I know I'll never forget the faces I saw, the hands I shook, and the lives I touched. They touched my life too. Each tour of "prison duty"—and there have been several—requires at least a month to get myself fully together again.

The Lord gives me other assignments which turn out to be a joy, revitalizing me and buoying me up for the tough times. Alternating with the series of appearances that takes me on the road, I try to schedule talks closer to home so I can be with my family.

Among my favorite audiences are the groups of ladies—Women Aglow and others—who open their arms and hearts to me even though they haven't a clear idea what bodybuilding is (much less, whether they approve of it!). In a different way, I have to prove myself to them too. But walking in laden with a barbell in each hand, a water bottle under my arm, and a steel rod over my shoulders isn't the way to do it. No, for the women, I leave my bag of tricks at home along with my gym trunks and tank top. They much prefer honest heart-to-heart dialogue with a guy dressed in a three-piece suit. And I'm happy to oblige.

Women are smart; they can spot a phony a mile away. They also know and appreciate a guy's sincerity. Whenever I tell my story to a group of ladies, I can relax, and let myself go, knowing that they understand. When I talk about my brush with cancer I sometimes feel as if I'm reliving the whole experience. The memories are so vivid, that I feel the pain and know the joy just as I did once before. I'm not ashamed that I've cried before my audiences. Tears can refresh and cleanse. I don't *plan* my talks to wring emotions from the audience or get spectators "charged up." If the mood is right and the words flow easily, people get involved. We might laugh together or cry together, but we always end up praying together. That's the bottom line.

Whereas my bodybuilding background serves a positive purpose in prisons and eventually gives me an entrance to talk about my faith, the opposite is true with most women's groups. After I've earned the ladies' confidence and respect through my sharing of spiritual beliefs, I will often introduce the subject of fitness. Beginning my talk by discussing diet and exercise might lose them immediately, but if I open with my testimony, I can close with a few pointers on feeling and looking good. Such tips are secondary, true, but I believe in *total* well-being—that means keeping ourselves physically, mentally, and spiritually healthy.

We're going to be more effective Christians and set better examples for others if we look good and feel good. So, if after my talk I'm asked to show a few exercises that will trim the waist or reduce the hips, I'm more than happy to loosen my tie and do just that.

Sometimes, when I notice ladies standing off the side and not participating in the impromptu exercise session, I go home wondering if I've offended them. Yet, in a day or two, I'll often receive a phone call or a note from those same bystanders asking what can be done to firm the upper arms or tighten chin muscles. I'm only sorry they didn't feel comfortable enough with our group to join in. I believe the Lord wants us to improve ourselves and to have fun while we're doing it.

I also believe the Lord wants us to keep our priorities in mind. First things first. As the full weeks passed, I slowly realized I was losing touch with mine. There were so many demands on my time, so many obligations. Road tours. Weekend speaking engagements. Christian TV talk show invitations. Telethons. Correspondence. Telephone calls. I felt myself torn between my ministry, my job, and my family.

Nancy seldom complained, but I knew she felt like she was sharing her husband with half the world. It was a throwback to my days in competition—only the "leftover" moments belonged to her. The cause was different but the effect was the same. Many evenings found us eating dinner at 11 P.M. or catching up on each other's news via long-distance phone calls at midnight.

Even when I was "home" I was in and out, here and there. Hours still were set aside for training sessions. After all, I had to keep fit in order to practice what I preached.

"You knew it would be like this when you married me, Nancy," I reminded her late one night as we shared another cold supper that she had prepared hours earlier.

"Yes, but . . ." came what had become the opening line for her arguments for my staying home more.

As I traveled the evangelistic circuit, I saw Christian witnesses so intent on helping others that their own home lives suffered. I couldn't let that happen to us. Nancy was far too important to me.

Our answer came in the form of a compromise. Unknown to the other, each of us had already been thinking and praying about the problem. The solutions we reached were in perfect harmony.

"I've decided not to complain about sharing you anymore," she told me one night. "There are a lot of people who need to hear you and meet you. The least I can do is to let you go without making you feel guilty. Maybe that sacrifice can be my way of saying 'thank you' to Jesus for healing you.''

My decision was to involve Nancy more in my ministry! She had never enjoyed a lot of bright lights and attention, but she did like one-on-one situations. I had begun to receive more and more requests to visit hospitals and homes where cancer patients were fighting battles similar to the one we had fought. Nancy could go with me and help me talk to these people and bring God's Word to them. Was she willing?

''Well, I'm willing to *try,*'' she answered thoughtfully.

Not only did she prove to be up to the job, but she doubled as a super support system for me. Visiting terminal patients can be depressing. So much suffering. So many tears. Yet the calls came daily, one on top of the other.

''Hello, Bill? You don't know me, but I saw you on the '700 Club' and wondered if you could come and see my mom. The doc says there's no hope and he's sent her home to die. Could you visit her? Please? We only live forty miles or so from Indianapolis.''

Often, at times like these we have arrived to find members of the family in tears, all hope gone, hovering over the sickbed, doling out medicine, and carefully maintaining a death vigil. These family members always mean well, and all their actions are motivated by love, but so often they're following the wrong course! Young children, full of energy and sunshine, are not allowed in the room to see grandma. Pleas go forth to the doctor for more and more medication to dull the senses and keep the patient in a state of woozy limbo.

Often Nancy will sit with the family and tell about our experience when she and mom and dad were in a similar situation. She emphasizes the importance of being hopeful and positive. The message I take to the patient is similar in essence to Nancy's.

I recall my own story and read Scriptures that explain God's healing power. As weak as the patient usually is, he often reaches out and grabs onto the possibility of life. I applaud this attitude and explain it's the first step to recovery. With the right kind of support, this spurt of strength can become more than a fleeting thing.

"God doesn't love me any more than He loves you," I'd challenge the patient. "Yet He healed me. And you can experience the same miraculous love and care that I did, whether in physical or spiritual healing."

For every victory, there were many defeats. Some came as no surprise. Occasionally, family members would call us to the bedside of a victim who truly didn't want to live. For whatever reason he'd rather die than fight. I am the last person on earth such a patient wants to see, challenging him to declare his belief in Jesus and telling him to take up his bed and walk.

To protect the privacy of people like that, I decided to stipulate that, if a patient wants me to come, he must extend the invitation, not a friend or relative. I don't want to coerce people into accepting my beliefs or force them to hear my story. For persons who live beyond my sphere of travel, I prepared a tape of my testimony in the hope that it might revive the dormant faith that can invite healing. Then it's up to the family and pastor to sustain and build that faith.

Sometimes the hope and promise of a miracle dies there. Too many people today find it difficult to apply the teachings of the Bible to current times. They let doubts get in the way of their faith. I don't blame them for their doubts, but I feel sorry for them. Those same doubts can prevent a miracle's taking place. Faith isn't something to stand on when life goes well, only to cast it aside when faced with terminal illness.

I believe God can heal anyone. He doesn't pick out

certain "lucky ones." It's up to the person. I think cancer patients can live, but it takes fight. It's often easier to die than be healed. With the drugs we have today, it is possible to die in relative comfort. It takes a lot of fight, and a big person to say, "No, I'm going to live."

Sometimes cancer has progressed so far that only a miracle from God can stop it. Very few people experience the type of miracle that I did. But God is powerful enough to take on even cancer and beat it.

Sometimes I'm asked if I believe in doctors. Absolutely! Doctors are necessary, but when an illness becomes "terminal" and the doctors say science can do nothing more, God has to take over completely. The Bible says to lay hands on the sick and they shall be healed. I'm a firm believer that God can heal everybody. He's a God of goodness. His Book is full of proof that He can make miracles, move mountains, win wars. Why can't we believe Him?

But let's not wait until we need Him desperately before we come to Him. In spite of all the dramatic testimonies we hear, we don't have to be faced with a life-or-death situation before we ask Him into our hearts. Some of the most devoted Christians I have known have fortunately never found themselves in dire circumstances. No terminal illness. No pending divorce. No alcohol addiction. No mental depression.

Sometimes Christian speakers imply that to be truly born again a person must sink to the depths and then be raised up, preferably accompanied by a drum roll, clap of thunder, or bolt of lightening. Such happenings are the fabric of great testimonies and dramatic film footage, but they aren't necessary to spirituality. This is what I try to point out in my own ministry.

Sometimes, especially with young people, all that is required is a little shove in the right direction. Kids need role models. If I can win their respect and influence them to keep their lives clean, set goals for themselves, and follow the teachings of Jesus, I've succeeded. And they will succeed too.

Being a Christian witness doesn't always mean taking the stage or speaking through a microphone. I don't have to be "on" to be a witness. The Lord occasionally gives me an assignment right in my own neighborhood, my hometown, or my home. I've been approached by guys in the gym and asked to share my experiences.

I never talk to them about drugs unless I am asked. Everyone knows I don't take steroids and that I don't believe in them. But preaching about my feelings to guys who do take the pills or injections would only make them uncomfortable and probably wouldn't stop their use of drugs anyway. They know my stand and if they want to talk, I'm willing to listen. Many have approached me, claiming they're curious about what happened to me. Usually, after they relax and open up, I find the real reason for the talk is much more serious—they've discovered a lump, a knot, or swelling. They're scared.

Probably the most important facet of my ministry takes place—not in a high school gym, a fellowship hall, or a prison cell—but in a blue Cape Cod house sitting high on a grassy hill and overlooking a little pond and a meadowful of horses. The audience is comprised of three shiny-faced boys, Kent, Stephen, and Jacob. As a parent, they are my greatest challenge and as a Christian, they are my greatest hope. Nancy and I witness to them daily, but in a far different way than we do for the public.

Stephen and Jacob are too young to really understand cancer, drugs, and the temptations that once caused their daddy to stray from the direction he knew was right. Someday I'll explain all that to them, but in the meantime, there are Scriptures to learn, verses to memorize, and children's Bible stories to teach. We make up games to play that test the boys' knowledge of the Bible and its characters. We sing songs that emphasize Jesus' love. We take turns saying grace before every meal. We have abbreviated bedtime prayer sessions that will expand with their attention span. The boys squirm a little, giggle a lot, pinch and tease each other. (I wonder where they learned those antics!) But they look to Nancy and me to set the pace and the example. Sometimes we measure up. Sometimes we fail.

My purpose for all this is simple: I'm trying to lay the kind of Christian foundation that my parents laid for me—the unshakable kind that's built to last. I hope Kent, Stephen, and Jacob never have to test their faith against terminal cancer, but if they do, I want to know they're fortified for the challenge. I was. Faith is the greatest gift my parents ever gave me. It was the gift of life.

Chapter 11

WINNING
THE NATURAL WAY

Several years ago I was asked to speak at a rural church in South Carolina. The pastor, my host for the day and one of the finest Christians I've ever met, had lost his wife to cancer a few months earlier. He was doing an excellent job of rearing his three beautiful kids himself.

I was so intrigued with the spiritual strength of the family that I spent most of the afternoon with the kids, showing the sons how to work out. One of the boys was particularly interested in bodybuilding and became my shadow, asking questions and seeking advice about training for competition. He was so enthusiastic that I was happy to share everything I knew. Recently his preacher dad called me long distance to tell me the boy's interest hadn't faded since our visit.

"Bill? I wanted you to be the first to know that Todd's competing in the Mr. Teen-age America contest next month," he said excitedly.

I knew he expected me to be thrilled, but I wasn't. In fact, I felt a little sick inside. I pray the boy isn't on drugs; but in national competition, all too often, the athletes succumb to the temptation. The unhappy truth is that the chances of winning without steroids are practically nonexistent. For that reason, I believe until the sport is cleaned up, it's not fit for kids.

Since winning the Mr. Indiana title in 1970, I've never again placed first in competition. Why? Because I'm clean. No drugs.

Oh, I've entered a few contests and have made a good showing, but I can't seem to compensate for the drug factor—the winner's edge. The little blue pills and the long steel needle are the difference between a first-place trophy and a runner-up ribbon. For the athlete trying to play by the rules, it's frustrating, maddening, and downright unfair.

Drugs are so prevalent in most bodybuilding contests that to give us clean athletes a chance, an annual non-drug competition has been devised on the West Coast. The title is "Mr. Natural America" and all entrants are required to submit to a blood test.

But even that contest has been tainted by drugs. In 1979, when I placed fourth, three entrants were scratched because they didn't pass the blood test. Even the winner was disqualified at the last minute. Nancy and I came home to Indiana so discouraged by the experience we decided I would drop out of competition completely until the sport is cleaned up.

Training the natural way—without drugs—is hard work. It's a sacrifice most athletes aren't willing to make. It takes time—years—to do it right. A lot of bodybuilders are in too much of a hurry. They don't want to wait for the real thing, so they go the drug route. Coaches encourage athletes to take the pills and try the injections. They want to win, too. When the spotlight of victory shines on a winner it's usually broad enough to include trainers, coaches, and managers as well. I don't condemn these guys for experimenting with drugs, but I'm concerned for them. I don't think they have any idea of the chances they're taking with their lives.

Weight lifters in the Midwest began popping pills during the fifties. Bodybuilders joined the trend a decade or so later. An excellent coach who guided me to many titles and trophies urged me to try steroids as part of my training regimen. He called them "miracle" drugs. And it certainly seemed that they were.

He had gotten them from doctors who worked out at the gym. These people weren't "pushers" trying to get guys hooked. They were merely naîve and were trying to help an athlete increase his ability by offering medication they really didn't understand.

Not long ago, I saw this same former coach at a contest I had entered. We hadn't seen each other for years and here I was, competing for another title. The day I can't hold my own against an open field is the day I'll retire.

"Bill, you look better than I've ever seen you," the coach said to me. This was a real compliment since he had known me during my drug days when I was winning every contest I entered. But in spite of my current fitness, we both knew that as long as I trained naturally, without the pills, I could never go up against the superstars.

"You know and I know that the pills make the difference," the coach said. "They're still a miracle drug."

I told him about my trip to the West Coast, the Mr. Natural America contest, and the drugs that are being used by "progressive" California bodybuilders. I also explained what happens to athletes who take too many pills for too many years. Although he had spent most of his life in a gym, he was amazed.

"You've told me more about drugs in these five minutes than I have ever known in my life," he said honestly.

He's not alone. Today, twenty years after drugs first became a factor in sports, few people really understand their danger. Why? Because a lot of athletes who suffer bad side effects merely "drop out" of the spotlight and are never heard from again. They don't want to stand up, admit they took drugs to win, and tell the world how they've suffered because of it.

A friend who trained with me for two years before he went on drugs, let his desire to win get the best of him. Once he became involved with steroids he ballooned out like those hot-water bottles I use in my stage program. He competed at 215 pounds and won a roomful of trophies before dropping out.

When I saw him last year, I was shocked to see that he looked like a little old man. He weighs 160 pounds and at thirty is losing his hair. He told me apologetically that his frail appearance was a consequence of his not training for six months.

But that's not a valid excuse. If I didn't go near a gym or a barbell for a year, my physique wouldn't change drastically from when I'm working out. The reason is that my muscle was developed through hard work. When you're clean, you're built to last.

Putting drugs into a human body is kind of like adding nitro to a carburetor. There is an immediate result that assures a great performance. But, almost as quickly, it burns out. A drug that causes muscle to grow that fast will cause equally swift deterioration when use is cut out. The natural way is the only way to achieve long-range benefits.

Occasionally, when someone hears I've been competing for over twenty years, he'll look at me in disbelief and ask my age. What does age matter? I'm in the best shape of my life. I can run the forty-yard dash better than when I was in high school. I feel no negative effects of age because I take care of myself.

Perhaps the saddest part of depending on drugs to win amateur contests is that the victors' only rewards for their efforts are a little hardware. They're willing to risk their health for a collection of tarnished trophies, faded ribbons, and titles that don't mean anything by comparison. At least in the pro ranks there is a money factor. And it's *big* money.

The purse at one of the best known bodybuilding contests is $50,000. Lesser shows award $10,000 to the winner. The pros start taking their drugs a few months before the lucrative contests and they stop taking them afterward. In this way they can hope to stay on the competitive scene for a few more years. Between contests they lose most of their muscle and power. When they're not on drugs, they are seldom seen in gym trunks and generally wear warm-up suits for public appearances and endorsements. They're embarrassed!

A good buddy of mine—an Indianapolis policeman—took a vacation trip to California with the idea of training in one of the well-known West Coast gyms. This is every bodybuilder's dream. While he was there he spotted a vaguely familiar face. He studied the man and finally realized he was one of the biggest names in our sport. He had won all the major titles and purses. My friend approached the "champ" and asked if he could take a snapshot as a souvenir.

"Hey, I don't mind your taking a picture," the bodybuilder said meekly. "But I'm nothing right now."

"Bill, I've seen eighth-graders look better than this guy did," explained my buddy later. "And he's a pro!"

The Lord doesn't want us to be two people—one remarkable on-stage presence and a second, lesser off-stage version. I believe He wants us to be the same men and women in the gym as we are in our offices, our homes, and our churches. The way to achieve this is to be honest, clean, and disciplined. Physical fitness and Christian witness should go together hand in hand. We're caretakers of the bodies God gave us. We should keep them healthy and trim. We make far better Christian examples when we're walking, talking evidence of discipline and moderation.

Bodybuilding isn't for everyone. Whenever I speak to a group of people—whether they're prison inmates, homemakers, young athletes, or members of a church fellowship—I urge them to get involved in a training program. Even if they have no desire to compete, I tell them to train natural and train to win and to choose a sport that suits their interests and their lifestyle and preferably, one the whole family can share.

Our three sons do not show serious interest in bodybuilding yet. However, they love the hours we spend together in our basement gym working out. Stephen already can bench press many pounds more than his body weight and can do ten chin-ups.

As we train side by side we talk. Actually, they talk and I listen—really listen. In this kind of setting a dad can get close to his kids, learn what concerns them, and spot any potential trouble before it develops. After a good workout, I send them off to the showers and then we congregate, tired and squeaky clean, for some quiet time—Bible study and devotions.

Nancy is a newcomer to our home gym but she has more enthusiasm than any of the rest. Yes, lifting weights is for women too. I can't think of a better way to tone muscles and spot-reduce. Women are becoming involved in shaping up through lifting weights. Many magazines are devoting pages to these female athletes and health clubs around the country are setting aside certain hours or certain days for women only. The end results are not unsightly bulging biceps, but firm, well-contoured bodies.

A doctor I know claims that American women over thirty-five are among the most physically unfit females in the world. About twenty-five million U.S. women are overweight and wear size sixteen dresses or larger.

Men seem to have a bit more luck keeping pounds off because they do it for health reasons, while women are apt to do it for appearances. I like to quote these facts whenever I address women's groups.

The Lord doesn't want His army of Christians to be fat, out of shape, and out of breath. How can we be representative of His Word if we let ourselves become so undisciplined? Often when I bring up these points in a discussion, I notice certain members of the audience shifting uncomfortably in their chairs, glancing from side to side for sister offenders, and even pushing away a dessert plate containing a half-eaten piece of pie or cake.

My purpose is not to cause embarrassment but to wake Christians up. Just as we have an obligation to Him to be spiritually fit, we also have a responsibility to be mentally and physically healthy. A program of combined regimens can achieve our goals. If we spend an hour or two a day stretching our minds by reading the Bible or inspirational books, we can take at least a few minutes each day stretching and expanding our bodies. Not only will physical appearances improve, this program will leave us more relaxed and with great spurts of energy to carry on His work. And feeling good about ourselves!

How to begin? Slowly and carefully. By making a game out of it if that helps. By considering oneself in basic training for God's army. New recruits or veterans can pledge themselves to a physical-mental-spiritual shape-up plan that includes time for devotions, exercise, study, and rest—and a training table diet too. Such a program can show the rest of the world what a winner—a Christian winner—looks and acts like. I am ready to volunteer as coach and share my game plan for winning the natural way.

POWERLIFTERS

For God hath not given us the spirit of fear; but of power, and of love, and of a sound mind.

2 Tim. 1:7

There's a joke—terribly old and not very funny—that goes like this: Some people exercise religiously; they do one push-up and say "Amen." Unfortunately, it's often true. Exercise is hard work, and not always fun.

But running or walking a mile on a beautiful fall morning can be an invigorating experience. With a temperature in the low sixties and nature's backdrop of fiery autumn colors, jogging down winding country roads can work out the kinks in the body and the problems in the mind.

Reading the Bible before starting the journey and mentally taking along a Scripture are other joys. Mulling it over, meditating on its various applications may just help find a meaningful place for it in life. By the time the runner rounds the last corner and returns to his own doorstep he'll feel tired, but energetic; peaceful, yet inspired to begin the day's work.

But what about the mornings that aren't sunny or cool and comfortable? What about an exercise regimen when it's raining, scorching hot, or even snowing? How about the days when the morning run seems endless because of the dampness that seeps into the bones and the chill that settles into the back and won't go away? What about the blisters? Callouses? Aching joints?

As we become more determined Christians, we realize that Jesus is not just a fair-weather friend, available only when life is easy. Nor is He merely a crutch to lean on during hours of need. He's devoted to us every hour of every day. He expects us to follow His example and be equally devoted to His way.

The rewards are practical as well as spiritual. A friend of mine who is a professor at a Big Ten university tells me that the medical bills of those who exercise are only half as much as for those who don't. The medical claims for sedentary men averaged $400 per year, while the claims for men who exercised three times a week were only $200 a year. This is solid evidence of the benefits of a well-structured fitness plan.

Not only does exercise add years to our lives, but it adds life to our years. A lot of stress evaporates in the gym, along the bike trail, in the swimming pool, or on the putting green. Physical fitness leads to mental fitness and they both contribute to spiritual fitness. Going for a long walk, doing a few stretching exercises, playing a set or two of tennis, or jogging is a good way to end a tension-filled day of work.

So is engaging in a favorite physical activity just until tired, but not exhausted; until the muscles tingle, but not ache, is the right way to do it. After a workout and a relaxing shower or bath is a good time to stretch out for some quiet time of devotions. Establishing and sticking with this pattern for two weeks can result in feelings that are more calm, more at peace with the world, and more in tune with God. Hopefully, this disciplined way of life will sell itself to the point of permanence.

God is my strength and power; and He maketh my way perfect.

2 Sam. 22:33

Being a Christian carries the responsibilities of will power, determination, and discipline. Self-indulgence is an ever-present temptation, but God gives us the strength to cope and the power to overcome.

Sometimes people eye me enviously and tell me how lucky I am not to have to worry about my weight. They're right. I don't waste time worrying about it; instead, I *do* something about it. I'm not naturally thin. I work at it. If I ate as much as I wanted, I'd gain thirty pounds within a few months. It's important to my ministry to weigh a fit 210, so I'm careful about my diet and I exercise daily.

Eating right and working out are the twin keys to weight control. Cutting down on food intake without exercising may take off pounds but will leave a person with slack muscles and flabby skin. Some heavyweights argue they'd rather exercise the pounds off than curb their eating habits. Their chances of success are slimmer than *they* are apt to be.

Like most homemakers, Nancy, who weighs 120 pounds, can burn up 240 calories while doing active housework for an hour. But if she stops for a light lunch of a hamburger and a glass of skim milk (447 calories,) she goes back to work with 207 calories still to be burned up.

Naturally, more vigorous activities use up more calories per hour. A few of the more beneficial energy burners are rapid bicycling (480 calories), ping pong (300 calories,) rowing (600 calories,) swimming (480 calories,) tennis (336 calories,) and sawing wood (372 calories.)

Unfortunately, working up a sweat also tends to work up an appetite. An hour on the ski slopes may consume

625 calories, but a couple of cups of steamy hot chocolate in front of the fire can diminish the benefits considerably. An hour on the golf links will burn 144 calories, but just one frosty glass of lemonade at the nineteenth hole negates those vigorous tee shots and the energy-draining putts.

It comes down to a numbers game. One pound of excess weight contains about 3,500 calories. To lose that pound, a person must consume 3,500 fewer calories than his body uses—500 fewer calories per day to lose a pound a week; 1,000 fewer calories per day to lose two pounds a week.

The numbers work in reverse too. If I had indulged myself with gooey ice cream treats during a recent Florida vacation, I could have easily come back four or five pounds heftier than when I left.

But I don't believe that's God plan for me. As His representative, I feel obligated to be the best person I can. Sometimes it's a sacrifice—sometimes it actually *hurts*—but He deserves the best from each of us.

He giveth power to the faint; and to them that have no might he increaseth strength.

Isa. 40:29

Traditionally, man has been thought of as the stronger sex, and over the years has been more apt to be concerned with keeping physically fit. Women, the "weaker sex," stayed home and took care of the kids and made sure things were running smoothly in the household.

Today, however, women are increasingly aware of keeping themselves physically fit. Gyms throughout the country today are full of women who are finding that the advantage of working out with weights is that they do not have to develop the bulging muscles that men do, but they can develop or reduce areas of their bodies.

My wife and her training partner, Uygonda, initially began their visits to the gym as a way of getting away from the daily routine. They started with a program of a few sit-ups, side bends, bicycle exercises, ending with a short session in the whirlpool.

But, as Nancy began to follow the advice I gave her concerning her exercise program, she was amazed to find the degree of improvement she was able to make in reducing or building up areas of her body.

Today, Nancy and Uygonda work out faithfully for two hours, three times a week. They find themselves spending less time in the steam room and the whirlpool and on the bicycle, because they are making use of such gymnastic equipment as the bench press, the Olympic sets, and the leg extension machine, and other exercises that women at one time would have not considered.

But, Nancy is walking proof that such a program works for women as well as for men.

That thy way may be known upon earth, thy saving health among all nations.

Ps. 67:2

You say you don't want to be a body builder? You say you don't know a medicine ball from a whiffle ball, and furthermore, you don't care to learn? Okay, okay, I've said it before and I'll say it again: bodybuilding and weight lifting aren't for everyone. This is the "do-your-own-thing" age and I'm all in favor of it. Now, what's your thing?

While you're trying to decide between racquetball, jogging, tennis, golf, polo (polo?), or shuffleboard, warm up the whole idea with leg raises and side bends. Start slowly, and gradually build your stamina. Be careful not to overtrain. Rotate your program so you're not doing the same exercises every day. Try a combination schedule—jog one day and swim the next.

Don't limit yourself to a seasonal sport. Golf is great, but unless you live in a warm climate you can't play in winter. Tennis is wonderful, but can you afford a membership in a year-round club? When trying to determine your "thing" take into consideration your life style and budget.

Whatever your decision, stick with it. Pledge yourself to a training regimen and don't give in or give out. Make exercise as much a part of your day as your morning glass of juice or your afternoon coffee break. Be strong for Him; be fit for Him; set a good example as one of His witnesses. Stand ready for any challenge He might present; accept any assignment He might give.

If you're not happy with the way you look, change it. Our God desires that you be the very best (for we are made in His image.)

Finally, my brethren, be strong in the Lord, and in the power of his might.

Eph. 6:10

When I take my message of Jesus Christ to an audience, I see myself cast in the role of a salesman—only instead of pushing ice cream or real estate, I'm promoting a way of life. I'm trying to convince listeners to hear and adhere to His Word and to invite the Lord into their hearts. I'm a living, breathing example of what He can do for a person.

People study me, scrutinize me, and look for imperfections before deciding whether or not to "buy" what I'm offering. If I claim that God can shoulder our cares and burdens, yet appear tense and unhappy, I surely won't make a sale. If I promise that the Lord can heal us and make us healthy, while I look out of shape and lack energy, I won't be very convincing.

I believe God wants us to be healthy and happy. He's entrusted us with a great deal of physical and mental potential and He expects us to develop this potential to its fullest. To make us stronger He's tossed obstacles in our way and then watched to see if we could overcome them.

I've had my share of low points—big and little obstacles—and I'm grateful for each one. They've taught me to grow and mature. A person who has everything handed to him seldom achieves much success in life. My small struggles over the years helped prepare me for my big fight. I'm grateful for my battle with cancer because it caused me to find my way back to Jesus and to a new, happier life.

When I go to speak today, my wife is with me. We talk about our spiritual life, which comes first. But we can also tell and illustrate the importance of man and wife and young persons taking care of their physical bodies and adding years to their lives and happiness to marriage or career. Through the talent God has given each of us, our ministry is as one. We go wherever the Lord leads us.

I think God wants His followers to be winners. He gave us His best and we can do likewise. Winners don't necessarily come equipped with titles, trophies, and ribbons, and they never take shortcuts to victory. I learned that the hard way. To be a winner in God's eyes, I believe we first have to earn our stripes in physical, mental, and spiritual fitness. This is an ongoing training program—a lifetime obligation. All that's required is determination, dedication, and discipline.